# THRUM HALLERS
## HALIFAX HEROES 1945-1998

# 100 GREATS

# THRUM HALLERS

## HALIFAX HEROES 1945-1998

COMPILED BY
ROBERT GATE

TEMPUS

*Champions 1985/86. From left to right, back row: Whitfield, Tony Anderson, Wilson, Riddlesden, Robinson, Scott, Bond, Dixon, James, Juliff. Front row: Crossley, Stephens, Chris Anderson, McCallion, Smith.*

*Frontispiece: Station Road, Swinton, 22 May 1965. Two of Halifax's all-time greats, Ken Roberts and John Burnett parade the Championship trophy after 'Fax's 15-7 victory over St Helens.*

*Front cover: Chris Anderson, Wembley 1987.*

*Back cover: Ken Dean (top), Karl Harrison (middle), John Burnett (bottom).*

First published 2004

Tempus Publishing Limited
The Mill, Brimscombe Port,
Stroud, Gloucestershire, GL5 2QG
www.tempus-publishing.com

© Robert Gate, 2004

The right of Robert Gate to be identified as the Author
of this work has been asserted in accordance with the
Copyrights, Designs and Patents Act 1988.

British Library Cataloguing in Publication Data.
A catalogue record for this book is available from the British Library.

ISBN 0 7524 3211 7

Typesetting and origination by Tempus Publishing Limited
Printed and bound in Great Britain

# Acknowledgements

I am grateful for the help and kindness of several individuals in the preparation and production of this book.

Most notably, Andrew Hardcastle, the Halifax club's official historian and author of several excellent works on the club, has proofread the manuscript, pointed out the errors of some of my ways where necessary, and filled in some of the gaps in the pictorial record.

John Furbisher, the Editor of the *Halifax Evening Courier*, kindly gave permission for the reproduction of material from that publication, which has diligently covered Halifax RL club and its affairs since its inception 130 years ago.

Andrew Cudbertson supplied the front cover illustration and other photographs, while others who have contributed in various ways are Andy Cole, the late Harold Farrimond, Charles Gate, Sig Kasatkin, Barry Rennison, Alex Service, Roger Shackleton, Andrew Wheelwright and Geoff Whippey.

*Coach Gareth Price addresses his team in 1959. Eleven of the fifteen men captured in this photograph appear as Great Thrum Hallers in these pages. From left to right, standing: Gareth Price, Jack Wilkinson, Colin Clifft, John Thorley, Les Pearce, David Fairbank, Wyn Phillips, Johnny Freeman, Brian Sparks. Kneeling: John Shaw, Alan Snowden, Alan Jarman, Billy Pratt, Garfield Owen, Ken Dean.*

# Introduction

Halifax last played a first-team fixture at Thrum Hall on 22 March 1998, when, hallelujah, Leeds were beaten 35-28 in a friendly. Sadly, the intervening years have not been kind, culminating in relegation from Super League in 2003 and, six years on, their new home at The Shay remains embarrassingly incomplete.

This book is a reminder and a celebration of 100 men, Great Thrum Hallers, who helped to light up many a post-war winter season at professional football's most elevated ground in the kingdom. They were not all great players, despite the book's title, but they were all notable and memorable in various ways.

Players were selected on the following criteria:

1. They had to have played a minimum of two seasons at Thrum Hall in the post-war period.
2. They had to have appeared at least 70 times (excluding substitutions) in the Halifax first team.

By those criteria players such as Arthur Bassett, Jim Bevan, Hudson Irving, Mel Meek, Fred Rule and Charlie Smith would have qualified but were essentially pre-war and wartime players and were consequently omitted. Equally, players from the post-1997 Super League seasons were not considered, unless they fulfilled the above criteria. I am sure a later researcher will eventually place their contributions to Halifax's history on record. The criteria also explain why such massive Halifax favourites as Asa Amone, Brian Juliff, Joe Kilroy, Geoff Robinson, Dave Watson and others fail to qualify. Personal favourites such as Martin Bella, Dave Busfield, John Dalgreen and Cavil Heugh simply did not play enough games to qualify despite their manifest talents.

It grieved me to have to omit a number of players, who could just as easily have been in rather than out of the selection. If 120 had been allowed then the following would also have qualified: Colin Clifft, Gary Divorty, Hugh Duffy, Dick Fairbank, Tony Garforth, Carl Gillespie, Don Hatfield, Roy Hawksley, George Kenny, Frank Mawson, Len Olsen, Kia Rika, Mick Snee, Derek Tudball and David Walton.

According to the scrum-halves' union, all rules are made to be broken. Consequently, there is one exception to the criteria. I have included George Standidge, the idol of the Scratching Shed, who only played 56 games for 'Fax, although he certainly packed at least 70 games worth of furiously entertaining action into them. If George had been left out, the consequences could have been dire.

# Hypothetically Speaking

Several people have asked me to name the best Halifax post-war XIII in the course of the preparation of this book. It's an impossibility, of course, fraught with prejudice and ignorance. Instead I have come up with some other types of teams based on watching the blue and whites since 1956. No doubt these will cause eyebrows to be raised, foreheads to be furrowed and my sanity to be questioned, but here goes.

**The Fast XIII:** Joe Kilroy; Mark Preston, Greg Austin, Dave Willicombe, Johnny Freeman; Ron Ryan or Bruce Burton, Paul Daley; Cavil Heugh, Paul Rowley, Paul Dixon, Granville Hoyle, Colin Dixon, Charlie Renilson

**The Tacklers XIII:** Graham Eadie; Duncan Jackson, John Burnett, Graham Garrod, Steve Smith; Mick Blacker, Gordon Baker; Geoff Robinson, John Shaw, Alan Wood, Alan Thomson, Colin Dixon, Ken Loxton

**The Grafters XIII:** Steve Smith; Peter Goodchild, Dave Cholmondeley, Derek Reeves, Brian Juliff; Barry Robinson, Terry Langton; Jack Scroby, Seamus McCallion, Keith Neller, Tony Garforth or Steve Bond, Mick Scott, John Pendlebury

**The Entertainers XIII:** Joe Kilroy or Ronnie James; John Bentley, Colin Dixon, Freddy Tuilagi, Wilf George; Dave Watson, Jackie Pycroft; Brendan Hill, John Dalgreen, George Standidge, Terry Fogerty, Paul Dixon, Dave Busfield

**Winners XIII:** Garfield Owen; Mark Preston, Greg Austin, Geoff Palmer, Johnny Freeman; Chris Anderson, Alan Marchant; Karl Harrison, Ian Foye, Ken Roberts, Colin Dixon, Terry Fogerty, Charlie Renilson

Any opposition would have problems with all those combinations but the Winners XIII looks to have everything. There is extreme pace in the three-quarters, guile at half-back and in the pack, and authority and backbone for when things get tough. Two other essentials are provided in a great goal-kicker in Garfield Owen and a hooker who would guarantee majority possession in Ian Foye.

*Champions 1964/65. From left to right, back row: Fogerty, Duffy, Scott, Dixon, Roberts, Todd, Freeman, Hardcastle, Renilson. Front row: Robinson, Jackson, James, Burnett, Scroby, Harrison, Daley.*

# 100 Club Greats

Alvin Ackerley*
Malcolm Agar
Chris Anderson*
Tony Anderson
Greg Austin
Gordon Baker*
Graham (Ben) Beevers
John Bentley
Dai Bevan
Jimmy Birts
Mick Blacker
Steve Bond
John Burnett*
Bruce Burton
Dave Callon
Dennis Chalkley
Dave Cholmondeley
Des Clarkson
Mike Condon
Terry Cook
Paul Daley
Arthur Daniels*
Phil Davies
Ken Dean*
Terry Dewhirst
Colin Dixon*
Paul Dixon
Graham Eadie
Albert Fearnley*
John Fieldhouse
Terry Fogerty*
Frank Fox
Ian Foye
Johnny Freeman*

Graham Garrod
Wilf George
Peter Goodchild
Harry Greenwood
Tuss Griffiths
Michael Hagan
Tony Halmshaw
Karl Harrison
John Henderson
Tony Hepworth
Brendan Hill
Granville Hoyle
Duncan Jackson
Neil James
Ronnie James*
David Jones
Alan Kellett
Stuart Kelley
Stan Kielty*
Terry Langton
Ken Loxton
Tommy Lynch*
Alan Marchant
John Martin
Seamus McCallion
Keith Neller
Mick O'Byrne
Garfield Owen*
Geoff Palmer
Les Pearce
John Pendlebury
Wyn Phillips
Graham Pitchforth
Alan Prescott

Mark Preston
Gareth Price
Dave Rayner
Derek Reeves
Charlie Renilson*
Ken Roberts*
Barry Robinson
Paul Rowley
John (Sammy) Sanderson
Derrick Schofield
John Schuster
Mick Scott*
Jack Scroby*
John Shaw
Steve Smith
Alan Snowden
Roy Southernwood
Brian Sparks
George Standidge
Gary Stephens
John Thorley*
Peter Todd
Ken Traill
Fereti (Freddy) Tuilagi
Keith Waites
Les White
Colin Whitfield
Jack Wilkinson*
Keith Williams
David Willicombe
Scott Wilson
Alan Wood

The twenty who appear here in italics occupy two pages instead of the usual one.

*Member of the Halifax Rugby League Hall of Fame.

# Alvin Ackerley
### Hooker, 1948-1958

**Previous club:** Workington Town

**Halifax debut:** 9 October 1948 v. Widnes

**Final Halifax appearance:** 4 October 1958
   v. Keighley

**Appearances:** 396

**Tries:** 13   **Goals:** 0   **Points:** 39

**Transferred to:** Hull Kingston Rovers

**Honours:** Cumberland, England, Great Britain

It is forty-six years since Alvin Ackerley last donned the blue and white hoops of Halifax and more than thirty years since his death, tragically early at only forty-six, in December 1973. His image is still fresh, however, in the memories of the thousands who used to throng Thrum Hall in the balmy days of the 1950s. Everyone remembers 'Ack', the squat hooker, who led arguably the most dominating pack Halifax have ever fielded, which is saying a great deal in view of the many mighty sixes that have served the club in its 130 years of existence.

Alvin was a genuine king of the scrums. He knew all the tricks of his trade and it was a rare occurrence for any of his teams to lose the battle for possession, which was so crucial in the days of contested scrummaging. He could win the ball fairly and squarely but he also knew all there was to know about loose-arms, swinging, handling in the scrum and getting his feet up first. In Alvin's days there could be up to fifty scrums a match involving strenuous activity, some skulduggery and not a little cheating, but at least it was the same for everyone! It helped, of course, that throughout his career with Halifax Alvin could rely on wily scrum-half Stan Kielty to put the ball exactly where he wanted it. It also helped that he had highly efficient prop forwards alongside him, such as Don Hatfield, Mike Condon, Len Olsen and latterly that great duo John Thorley and Jack Wilkinson.

However, Alvin was more than a prodigious ball-winner. He was a force in the loose, scurrying about at the play-the-balls, shaking off tackles, putting in grubber-kicks, dummying and generally geeing up his men to greater efforts. He was as tough as old boots, led from the front and was never one to shirk the hard grind. His record of playing in over 600 first-class fixtures is shared by only three other hookers in the history of rugby league – an eloquent testament to his skills, fitness and durability.

Alvin was a Cumbrian from Dearham and he came from a rugby-playing family. He began his amateur career with Broughton Moor, had a trial for Barrow at seventeen in April 1945 and joined Workington Town in their inaugural season, 1945/46. Alvin was capped by Cumberland when he was not yet nineteen – practically embryonic for a hooker in that period. After playing 72 games for Workington, Alvin fell out with player-manager Gus Risman and went to play for amateurs Brookland Rovers.

Halifax paid Town £750 for him in October

*Alvin Ackerley leads out his team against Warrington at Wembley in the drawn Challenge Cup final of 1954.*

1948 and he went on to give a decade of brilliant service. In his first season he was a big factor in Halifax's shock run to Wembley. Indeed their 1949 cup final opponents Bradford Northern were said to be worried about just one thing – Alvin's ability to monopolise the ball. Their coach Dai Rees, a former 'Fax forward, pulled a master stroke, reinstating the giant prop Frank Whitcombe to disrupt the Halifax front row. Alvin hardly saw the ball, never mind hooked it. Bradford won the scrums 42-13 and the game 12-0. It was probably the biggest hiding Alvin ever took in the scrums.

Halifax rose to the heights in the 1950s, Alvin's ball-winning being a huge advantage. He was Cumberland's regular choice, winning sixteen caps between 1946 and 1959, although strangely he was never the county captain. Soon enough he was an England international, earning the first of 6 caps in a 31-18 victory over Other Nationalities at Wigan on 23 April 1952. In 1952/53 he played in games against Wales, Other Nationalities and France, while in 1953/54 he figured in victories over Wales and France as England won the International Championship. He was also in the Great Britain team which beat Australia 19-6 in the First Test of 1952 but did not play another Test until 1958. Amazingly, he was left out of the 1954 Lions tour when at the height of his powers. He was, however, selected for the 1954 World Cup party to France but had to decline. His selection for the 1958 tour was

well deserved but he was not the power of old.

Alvin's halcyon days were between 1952 and 1956, when he was synonymous with the Halifax captaincy. He took over the role from Arthur Daniels early in the 1952/53 season and proceeded to lead his team to the Championship final, losing to St Helens, and to the Yorkshire League Championship. With only a break for a time from November 1954, when Tuss Griffiths took over, Alvin remained in charge until the close of the 1955/56 season. He took Halifax to further Yorkshire League Championships in 1953/54 and 1955/56 and to Yorkshire Cup victories in 1954/55 and 1955/56, both against Hull. In the 1954 final he scored one of his 13 tries for Halifax, his first for two years and 82 games.

In 1953/54 he had the mortification of leading 'Fax to the game's two major finals, only to lose both narrowly to arch rivals Warrington – 4-8 in the Odsal Replay and 7-8 in the Championship final at Maine Road. Even more agonisingly, the same thing happened again in 1955/56 as Halifax came near to winning all four cups, only to lose to St Helens at Wembley after a scoreless first sixty-eight minutes, and then to a last-gasp penalty goal against Hull at Maine Road. That game was Alvin's last as Halifax's skipper, although he played for the club for another two years, picking up a fourth Yorkshire League winners' medal in 1957/58.

Sadly his Halifax career ended after a disagreement with coach Dolly Dawson, both leaving Thrum Hall as a result.

# Malcolm Agar
### Centre, 1981-1985

**Previous club:** Dewsbury

**Halifax debut:** 16 August 1981 v. Bradford Northern Yorkshire Cup

**Final Halifax appearance:** 4 September 1985 v. Widnes

**Appearances:** 126 + 7 subs

**Tries:** 42   **Goals:** 335 + 28 drop goals

**Points:** 843

**Transferred to:** Batley

Malcolm Agar cost Halifax a club record fee of £15,000 in 1981. He was signed specifically as a goal-kicker to replace Jimmy Birts, who had left for Wigan. He certainly succeeded, as 363 goals in 133 appearances was the result. Malcolm was a left-footed kicker with a penchant for landing goals from the touchlines and in crucial moments. He could certainly land long shots too, as anyone who saw one particularly spectacular goal from well inside his own half at Rochdale's old Athletic Grounds could testify.

As for kicking under pressure, his goal against Barrow at Thrum Hall on 10 October 1982 would take some beating. Halifax had lost the first eight games of the season and trailed Barrow 10-15 in the last minute, when Graham Garrod scored at the pavilion corner. Agar's touchline conversion was delayed while a Halifax player received attention and then a dog got onto the pitch and delayed the kick by another couple of minutes. Everyone's nerves were frayed except Malcolm's, who calmly slotted a magnificent conversion.

Malcolm had begun playing with Yorkshire Copperworks RU before signing for Dewsbury, for whom he had amassed 340 points in 116 appearances. Apart from his goal-kicking, Malcolm was a smart, quick-thinking player, who added a certain unpredictability to the three-quarter line. He had an eye for an opening and was a regular try-scorer.

In his first season at Thrum Hall Halifax won promotion. Malcolm made a considerable contribution with 269 points (16 tries, 102 goals, 17 drop goals). No other player in the game landed more drop goals than Malcolm that season. He played in 33 of Halifax's 34 games and failed to score just once, at Carlisle. On 11 April 1982 he scored 26 points (10 goals, 2 tries) in a 38-10 home victory over Huddersfield.

Although Halifax were relegated in 1982/83 Malcolm played in all 34 games, clocking up 143 points, his lowest total as a Thrum Haller. He had the distinction of registering Halifax's last three-point try, against St Helens at Thrum Hall on 10 April 1983. The following season saw Halifax promoted again, Malcolm piling up 234 points, including a rare double hat-trick (3 tries and 3 goals) and all Halifax's points in an 18-6 win at Rochdale.

Halifax tried Malcolm at full-back and wing in 1983/84, and in 1984/85 he played 15 of his 31 games at wing and three at full-back, as Chris and Tony Anderson arrived to fill the centre spots. Malcolm was still indispensable for his kicking, and that was a major factor in Halifax reaching the semi-finals of the John Player Trophy, when he kicked two goals in an 8-14 loss to Hull KR. Malcolm's career ended with spells at Batley and Bramley and with a final points tally of 1,246.

# Chris Anderson
Stand-off, 1984-1987

**Previous club:** Hull Kingston Rovers

**Halifax debut:** 2 December 1984 v. Castleford Players Trophy

**Final Halifax appearance:** 2 May 1987 v. St Helens Challenge Cup final

**Appearances:** 90 + 2 subs

**Tries:** 22   **Goals:** 0   **Points:** 88

**Transferred to:** Retired

**Honours:** New South Wales, Australia

No more popular or influential figure has emerged in Halifax's rugby league existence over the past two decades than Chris Anderson. Chris was a Thrum Haller for less than four years but for a whole generation of 'Fax fans no one will ever be more fondly remembered. David Brook, the Halifax president responsible for his appointment in 1984, never did the town or the club a better turn. For a few brief years Halifax were once again top of the pile.

Chris arrived at Thrum Hall in the deep winter of 1984. His best days were supposed to be well behind him. He had been a world-class wingman – quick, determined, agile, resolute and a deadly finisher, despite being on the small side at only 5' 7" and 11st 7lbs. His CV as a player was impressive. He had been a Kangaroo in 1978, playing in all five tests against Britain and France, and again in 1982 with 'The Invincibles', when he did not make the Test teams. He had won 8 Test caps in all and had been a member of the Australian team which won the World

Championship in 1975. He represented New South Wales 8 times, including four State of Origins, one of which was the inaugural match of the series. His senior club rugby had been with Canterbury Bankstown (1971-84), for whom he had claimed a record 94 tries in 232 appearances. He scored a record 19 tries in 1983 and played in three Grand Finals (1974, 1979 and 1980).

He had, simply, done it all. He had also played for Widnes during the 1974/75 season, grabbing 18 tries in 19 games. He played for the Chemics in their 2-3 loss to Bradford Northern in the Players Trophy final and was regarded so highly that Widnes flew him back from Australia to play at Wembley, when they defeated Warrington 14-7. Ironically, he scored three tries against Halifax in Widnes's 19-3 victory on 22 December 1974 – the only hat-trick he ever scored at Thrum Hall.

Chris had originally joined Hull KR in 1984 but only played twice for them before decamping for Halifax, who had won promotion the previous season and were heavily afflicted with the yo-yo syndrome. A further disadvantage was the fact that he displaced another great man of Halifax rugby league, Colin Dixon, who had certainly not deserved to be dumped. Chris would be judged harshly if he failed. The record shows that he more than fulfilled all expectations.

Amazingly, Chris never played on the wing for Halifax. He began at full-back and soon moved to centre but surprised everyone by

*Chris Anderson, extreme left, looks on as St Helens half-back Brett Clark is upended by Graham Eadie at Wembley in 1987.*

taking up the crucial role of stand-off in a sizzling 12-12 home draw with Wigan on 13 March 1985. Although he looked uncomfortable in the early stages of his acquaintance with this new position, he soon won over the sceptics. He was just brilliant – so effective, in fact, that some wondered why he had wasted all those years on the wing. He retained some of that devastating speed, particularly over a short distance, could find the gaps, was an outstanding organiser and tactician and was a firm tackler. It was, however, his obvious qualities as a leader which marked him out. He made others play. The sum of the teams he led at Thrum Hall was always greater than the total of their individual talents. Team spirit, determination and bloody-mindedness oozed out of his sides and they played good football. Tactically, he made them do things against the book, such as kicking from the scrum or on the first tackle and running the ball on the sixth.

In 1984/85 Chris had the satisfaction of keeping Halifax's motley combination of Aussies and locals in the First Division and of taking them to the Players Trophy semi-final. The 1985/86 season was a massive triumph for the Australian, who took a very underrated Halifax team to the Championship. Many games were won late and some seemingly through collective willpower. The sole disappointment was the failure to add the Premiership to the Championship. Chris was deservedly rewarded with the 1986 'Man of Steel' Coach of the Year award.

He began the 1986/87 season by taking the Man of the Match award in Halifax's Charity Shield victory over Castleford and ended it by leading Halifax to their first Challenge Cup since 1939, a glorious end to his playing career. As coach he took them back to Wembley in 1988 only to suffer defeat against Wigan. Returning to Australia, he coached Canterbury (1995) and Melbourne (1999) to Grand Final successes and was appointed coach to the Kangaroos in 1999, guiding them to World Cup triumph in 2000 and Ashes victories in 2001 and 2003.

# Tony Anderson
Centre, 1984-1990

**Previous club:** Brisbane Easts

**Halifax debut:** 30 September 1984 v. Hunslet

**Final Halifax appearance:** 11 March 1990
   v. Rochdale Hornets

**Appearances:** 143 + 2 subs

**Tries:** 66  **Goals:** 0  **Points:** 264

**Transferred to:** Oldham

One of the very first of the Australian invaders of Thrum Hall in 1984, Tony Anderson proved to be the longest-serving and most loyal of all the antipodeans who have come to Halifax over the last two decades. The fact that he is still here after twenty years is a testimony to his staying power and affection for the town and club. Tony ('TA') was first-team coach from September 2002 until April 2004, in very difficult times for the club but has had a variety of roles with Halifax over the years, including Alliance Team coach and junior development officer.

Tony made his debut as a half-time substitute for Andy Dickinson in a 32-18 win against Hunslet along with his Brisbane Easts teammate Martin Bella. Two weeks later he scored the first of 66 tries for 'Fax in a 23-16 home victory over Leigh. In that first season he played mainly at left-centre but swapped to right-centre the following season, when he proved potent in Halifax's annexation of the Rugby League Championship, scoring 11 tries in 34 games. Three of those tries came in the Premiership wins over Hull and Leeds but he had to be content with a runners-up medal, when Warrington beat Halifax in the Premiership final.

Quota restrictions prevented Tony from playing almost the entire 1986/87 season, as Grant Rix took his place but he was back at full throttle in the 1987/88 season. He played in the Charity Shield on the Isle of Man against Wigan and jointly topped the Halifax try-scorers list with Paul Dixon on 17 tries. Halifax went to Wembley in 1988 and Tony certainly played his part in getting them there. He claimed hat-tricks in the first two rounds against Heworth and Rochdale Hornets. In the semi-final replay at Elland Road against Hull he scored the all-important try, which won the tie 4-3, and he was again a try-scorer in the final against Wigan.

In the relegation season of 1988/89 Tony was top try-scorer with 13 and, along with Dick Fairbank, played most games (32). In January 1989 he took over the captaincy when Paul Dixon was transferred. When he played at full-back in a Challenge Cup-tie at Warrington on 29 January, he became one of an elite band of players who have figured in every back position for Halifax. Centre is, however, where he will always be remembered. He was extremely quick on attack but, remarkably, appeared even quicker in defence, often running down the fastest of opponents in try-saving chases.

He began his final season as captain, despite the introduction of player-coach John Dorahy, and he helped 'Fax reach the semi-finals of the Yorkshire Cup and the Regal Trophy final. On 1 October 1989, playing at stand-off, Tony scored four tries in a 72-20 victory at Nottingham City – his biggest try-haul for the club.

# Greg Austin
Left-centre, 1990-1993

**Previous club:** Hull KR

**Halifax debut:** 23 September 1990 v. Bramley

**Final Halifax appearance:** 4 April 1993
   v. Widnes

**Appearances:** 88 + 1 sub

**Tries:** 100   **Goals:** 2   **Points:** 404

**Transferred to:** Keighley

Greg Austin was that extremely rare creature, the natural try-scorer. Scoring tries seemed to be compulsive for Greg at every club he served. In an English career which stretched from 1985 to 1996, the Sydney-born centre racked up 274 tries in only 282 appearances, a scoring rate to which only the most prolific of wingers dare aspire. Most wingers could not keep up with Greg Austin. His eye for an opening was phenomenal and if a try was in the offing it was certain that Greg would sniff it out. He had a fine swerve and so much pace that he could go through the gap or round the man. Opposing centres had a tough job deciding whether to take Greg or cover the wing. Often they decided too late.

Greg arrived at Halifax in September 1990 after Hull KR decided to free up a quota place for the New Zealand Test prop James Goulding by releasing a centre, who had scored 45 tries in 38 appearances and helped them to win the Second Division Championship in 1989/90. That was Halifax's good fortune.

He made a try-scoring debut for Halifax as a substitute in a 56-8 win at Bramley. Thereafter it was tries all the way. In his fourth game for the club he bagged four tries in a record 82-8 home win over Runcorn Highfield. In his seventh game he scored his eighth try for Halifax against his compatriots as Halifax gave the Australians a hard time before succumbing 18-36. Against Trafford Borough on 7 April 1991 he ran in six tries to equal the record for a Second Division game, Halifax winning 66-26. By the season's end he had broken the record for a Halifax centre

with 40 tries in 30 games. Halifax had won promotion and been runners-up to Salford in the Second Division Premiership.

The following season he played in all 33 of Halifax's fixtures, claiming 33 tries and forming a highly productive combination with winger Mark Preston. His best haul was five against his old club Hull KR, who were butchered 76-8 at Thrum Hall, while he scored hat-tricks against Swinton (home and away) and against Barrow (home).

In his final season, 1992/93, he claimed 27 tries in 26 games, notching five against Nottingham City in another Regal Trophy tie. When he missed Halifax's game at Leeds on 18 December 1992, a run of 54 consecutive appearances came to an end. Apart from being a ruthless finisher, he remained remarkably free of injury. In his final game for Halifax he registered his 100th try for the club in only 89 appearances. Only Johnny Freeman (86 games) achieved a faster century for Halifax.

Among his later feats was 52 tries for Huddersfield in 1994/95, equalling Paul Newlove's all-time record for a centre. He also scored nine tries against Blackpool Gladiators, a Regal Trophy record.

# Gordon Baker

Scrum-half, loose forward, 1964-1982

**Previous club:** Kirkholt ARL

**Halifax debut:** 2 September 1964
*v.* Wakefield Trinity

**Final Halifax appearance:** 4 April 1982
*v.* Carlisle

**Appearances:** 262 + 42 subs

**Tries:** 60   **Goals:** 0   **Points:** 180

**Transferred to:** Rochdale Hornets

Gordon Baker was not the quickest, most elusive or trickiest scrum-half to have played for Halifax. He was, however, one of the bravest, most durable and hard-working. In all, he played for a period of almost eighteen years for the club – allowing for a three-year break – one of the longest careers on record for a Thrum Haller.

Gordon's stock-in-trade was all-out effort. Tackle counts had not been invented when he played but fans, players and coaches did not need statisticians to tell them that the scrum-half with the long fair hair always did more than his share of the tackling. There is little doubt that if he had been a few stones heavier and a few yards faster Gordon would have made his mark in representative rugby. As it was, he often did play at loose forward in his later years, while he had occasionally turned out at stand-off and centre. He was especially adept at stealing the ball, a valuable asset when his team's forwards were being beaten for possession.

A native of Rochdale, Gordon signed for Halifax towards the close of the 1963/64 season for a £450 fee. He marked his first-team debut with a crucial try in a 10-6 home victory over Wakefield Trinity but had to

bide his time in the 'A' team as Paul Daley and, subsequently, Jackie Pycroft stood in his way. At the tail end of 1965/66 Gordon suddenly found himself in the first team as Daley was crocked. He played brilliantly with Barry Robinson as his stand-off in the last seven games of the campaign. Included were the four play-off games which culminated in Halifax's second consecutive Championship final against St Helens at Swinton. Gordon scored five tries in those play-offs, including one in the final.

Gordon was 'A' team Player of the Year in 1965/66 but did not cement a secure place in the first team until 1967/68. For the following eight seasons he was a mainstay of a team which often struggled. In 1971/72, however, a glorious interlude occurred, when Gordon led Halifax to a wonderful triumph in the John Player Trophy final over Wakefield Trinity at Odsal. It was his greatest moment as a Halifax player and a few months later he was in the team which lost to Leeds in the semi-final of the Challenge Cup.

He won the Player of the Year trophy in 1973/74, when he succeeded Terry Fogerty as club captain. In 1975 his benefit realised a club record £2,174 but in 1976 he was released to Rochdale Hornets on a free transfer, subsequently moving to Leigh. He returned to Halifax in 1978/79 and played another four years for 'Fax, mostly in the reserves. His last game for Halifax was just before his thirty-seventh birthday but he carried on playing amateur rugby for New Hey well into the 1990s.

# Graham (Ben) Beevers
Prop, 1980-1990

**Previous club:** Ovenden ARL

**Halifax debut:** 19 October 1980 v. Castleford

**Final Halifax appearance:** 25 November 1990 v. Barrow

**Appearances:** 108 + 33 subs

**Tries:** 2  **Goals:** 0  **Points:** 8

**Transferred to:** London Crusaders

While all fans appreciate having star players in their teams, they also admire the workhorses without whom the stars would struggle. They like it even more when such players are local lads. Ben Beevers was Halifax through and through. He was a native of the town and played rugby league for Halifax Catholic High School before moving on to play as an amateur for Ovenden. He signed for Halifax in July 1980 when he was nineteen and went on to give Halifax great value for a decade.

Ben began as a second-rower but did not really have the pace for the position. He excelled, however, as a front-row man. His was a no-frills style. He was a workaholic tackler, prepared to drive the ball up all day, never shirked a challenge and never knew when he was beaten. He scored only twice for Halifax and probably played as often for the reserves as for the first team. He will always be remembered though for his spirit, belligerence and loyalty by Thrum Hall followers and he won more tangible honours than many more famous players who have played for Halifax.

His debut as a substitute in a 9-23 defeat at Castleford marked the end of Johnny Blair's brief career with Halifax and was shared by three other debutants in Graham Hirst, Dave Potts and Nigel Whitehouse. His first full appearance did not occur for almost another eighteen months, when he shared the second row with Alan Shillito in a 14-8 win at Blackpool Borough on 7 March 1982. By that season's close he had made 11 appearances and helped Halifax to gain promotion. He made 13 appearances in Halifax's next promotion season two years later and did not finally cement a regular first-team place until 1984/85, when he became the regular number ten.

In 1985/86 he had the misfortune to suffer a hernia injury and missed most of the Championship-winning campaign but did make enough appearances to qualify for a medal. The following season did not see him make his first appearance until 29 October 1986 against the Kangaroos. He soon established himself at blind-side prop, however, and was a tower of strength in Halifax's triumphant Challenge Cup campaign, giving everything he had at Wembley before being replaced by Neil James for the final thirteen minutes. His performances throughout the season earned him the Tetley Trophy, the club award for consistency.

Despite playing in 22 games in 1987/88 and appearing in the Charity Shield against Wigan, Ben missed out on the club's second Wembley run, falling behind Keith Neller, Neil James and Dick Fairbank in the prop pecking order. A broken arm at St Helens in December 1988 blighted the latter part of his career, his last big match being a thrilling affair against the Australians in 1990, when Halifax lost 18-36. Ben enjoyed a successful benefit in 1990.

# John Bentley
Right-winger, 1992-1998

**Previous club:** Leeds

**Halifax debut:** 6 September 1992 v. Leeds

**Final Halifax appearance:** 17 July 1998
v. Sheffield Eagles

**Appearances:** 132 + 3 subs

**Tries:** 109   **Goals:** 1   **Points:** 438

**Transferred to:** Huddersfield

**Honours:** England, Great Britain

As a crowd-pleaser John Bentley has had few superiors at Thrum Hall. Not many players develop an almost symbiotic relationship with the fans and the ones who do always remain in the memories of those who watched them. A few who spring to mind are Colin Dixon, George Standidge, Wilf George and Geoff Robinson and, without doubt, John Bentley, affectionately known as 'Bentos'.

It was not surprising that the Thrum Hall faithful took to John, although they were not too keen on him when he was a Loiner. John had that extra something. He was strong, fast and physical but he was also mesmeric when it came to running in a broken field. He had the swerve, acceleration, determination and instinct to find the right angles of running, which enabled him to score some truly fantastic tries. He was also capable of making errors but that did not put off the fans, who knew he would do his damnedest to make up for them. His enjoyment of the game was unmistakable.

John had played amateur rugby league but made his name in union, playing for Cleckheaton, Otley and Sale before attaining England status in 1988. Shortly afterwards, Leeds tempted him into league with a reported signing-on fee of £80,000. In four seasons at Headingley he won many admirers, played 101 games, bagged 53 tries and was capped by Great Britain against France in 1992 but only gained a runners-up medal for the 1992 Regal Trophy, as Leeds failed to take major honours.

Halifax signed John in a complicated deal which involved £100,000 and hooker Seamus McCallion going to Headingley, with John and loose forward Gary Divorty coming in the opposite direction. His first eight games for 'Fax were played at right-centre to Henry Sharp but he was soon providing huge entertainment on the wing, 1992/93 bringing 20 tries in 29 games. The following season he was partnered by John Schuster and finished as the leading try-scorer with 25 in 32 matches, while he did even better in 1994/95 with 29 tries in 33 appearances, including one against the Australians.

John won a second Test cap against France in 1994, played for Great Britain in the Sydney Sevens and spent the summer playing for Balmain, while in 1995 he represented England in the World Cup.

In the shortened 1995/96 Centenary season he shared top spot with Mike Umaga on 10 tries, including four against Sheffield Eagles. The first Super League campaign of 1996 was his last full season at Thrum Hall and yielded 22 tries in 21 games. He scored four tries twice, against London Broncos and, joyously, against Leeds. The 1997 and 1998 seasons saw him play only eight games as injuries and a dual career in rugby union interfered. His star quality shone through in union, as he again won England honours and was a star turn on the 1997 British Isles tour of South Africa.

# Dai Bevan
Left-winger, 1953-1956

**Previous club:** Wigan

**Halifax debut:** 12 December 1953 v. York

**Final Halifax appearance:** 17 April 1956
v. Batley

**Appearances:** 101

**Tries:** 34   **Goals:** 0   **Points:** 102

**Transferred to:** Retired

**Honours:** Wales, Great Britain

David Royston Bevan was born in Penycraig, Tonypandy in 1928 and played rugby union for the local grammar school before migrating north. His rugby union career continued with Oldham RU Club from where he joined the old, lamented Belle Vue Rangers as a twenty-year-old wingman. He spent four years with the Rangers, scoring 48 tries in 130 games. Wigan recognised his talents and paid Rangers £2,000 for his signature in 1952. He arrived in time to help them win the Lancashire League title and take the Championship, although he did not play in the final.

In 1952/53, his only full season at Central Park, Dai scored 38 tries in 43 games and won caps for Wales against Other Nationalities and for Great Britain against Australia, coming in for the Third Test when Arthur Daniels dropped out. The following season he helped Wigan reach the Lancashire Cup final, scoring their only try in the semi-final against Leigh, but again did not figure in the final.

Halifax had a problem filling their left-wing spot following the retirement of Terry Cook and decided that Dai Bevan was an ideal replacement, paying Wigan £1,700 for his services in December 1953. He arrived at a good time as Halifax ended up top of the league, won the Yorkshire League Championship and contested the Challenge Cup and Championship finals in 1953/54. Dai played in the Warrington trilogy at Wembley, Odsal and Maine Road, snuffing out Warrington's major threat, Brian Bevan.

Indeed, while with Halifax at least, Dai was renowned for his defensive prowess rather than his attacking skills. Many thought him the best defensive wingman in the game.

Halifax had not bought Dai for his tackling – he was very quick and determined and had scored almost 100 tries for Belle Vue and Wigan – but it took him nine games to score his first try for Halifax, against Hull KR on 27 February 1954, and he only claimed 3 in 23 games in his debut season. His rate picked up in 1954/55 when he scored a dozen and he was in Halifax's Yorkshire Cup-winning team against Hull. Opposing three-quarters had a hard time scoring against Halifax's left-wing pairing of Dai and Peter Todd, another tough tackler.

Dai's final season was 1955/56 when he had a new centre partner in Geoff Palmer. Dai scored 19 tries, including a hat-trick in a 44-7 romp against Castleford at Thrum Hall. He played in Halifax's thrilling 18-17 victory over the Kiwis and claimed important tries in Yorkshire Cup-ties against Wakefield Trinity (second round), Castleford (semi-final) and in the drawn final against Hull at Headingley, picking up his second winners' medal after Halifax's 7-0 victory in the replay at Odsal. He also collected a second Yorkshire League medal and runners-up medals for the Championship and Challenge Cup, although Johnny Freeman was preferred for the finals.

# Jimmy Birts
Full-back, 1978-1981

**Previous club:** Bradford Northern

**Halifax debut:** 5 March 1978 v. Huyton

**Final Halifax appearance:** 20 April 1981
    v. Hull Kingston Rovers

**Appearances:** 102

**Tries:** 15   **Goals:** 272 + 15 drop goals

**Points:** 604

**Transferred to:** Wigan

**Honours:** Great Britain Colts

Halifax were in desperate straits when Jimmy Birts arrived at Thrum Hall on a month's loan from Bradford Northern in February 1978. Halifax were bottom of the league and had lost all twenty-four games played, including the infamous John Player Trophy tie against Cawoods. Newly installed coach Maurice Bamford knew how good Jimmy Birts could be if given the chance. At Odsal his path was barred by the incomparable Keith Mumby and Jimmy had only played one first-team game for Northern – on the left wing.

On his debut for Halifax at Huyton he announced his arrival by landing a forty-five-yard penalty after twelve minutes, finishing with three goals in a 13-5 victory – perhaps the longest-awaited win in the club's history. In his next game against York he broke his thumb and his season ended. Halifax knew they wanted him but were so cash-strapped that they could not raise the £2,000 fee. He was signed at last six months later for £1,500.

Jimmy became a leading figure in Halifax's near-miraculous resurrection over the next three years. Red-haired, six feet tall but slimly-built, Jimmy Birts was as good an all-round full-back as has been seen at Thrum Hall. He was capable of landing goals from halfway and beyond and was adept at dropping goals, while his tackling was of the textbook variety. His attacking style was exciting, his long dashes being executed at considerable pace and he registered some spectacular tries.

In his first full season, 1978/79, Jimmy played in all 33 of Halifax's games, landing goals in 30 of them, amassing 178 points (86 goals, 2 tries). Against Hull KR at Thrum Hall in a Floodlit Trophy tie he kicked six goals in a 12-21 defeat, an unprecedented feat in a match when no try had been recorded by Halifax.

In 1979/80 he racked up 223 points, including 10 tries, as Halifax reached the Yorkshire Cup final. Jimmy scored all Halifax's points in a 6-25 defeat by Leeds, including two monstrous early penalty goals. He also played a large part in taking Halifax to the Challenge Cup semi-finals and to promotion to Division One.

His last season at Halifax, 1980/81, saw his team wage a valiant but unsuccessful battle against relegation. Jimmy contributed 195 points to the cause in 32 appearances. Four minutes from the end of the last game of the season he kicked his seventh goal in a 30-16 victory over Hull KR. It was his 100th of the season, 14 of which had been drop goals.

To the consternation of Halifax fans, two months later Jimmy transferred to Wigan, now coached by Maurice Bamford, for £22,000. He only played 11 games for Wigan, injury and bad form hastening his subsequent transfer to Carlisle for £12,000. Wigan might have lost a packet on the deal but Halifax's loss was greater.

**Previous club:** Bradford Northern

**Halifax debut:** 11 February 1978 v. Leeds

**Final Halifax appearance:** 2 January 1983
   v. Hull Kingston Rovers

**Appearances:** 130 + 11 subs

**Tries:** 33   **Goals:** 1 + 1 drop goal

**Points:** 102

**Transferred to:** Warrington

**Honours:** Yorkshire

Halifax have been fortunate to have had some inspirational players over the years. Mick Blacker fits firmly in that category. There is not much doubt that Maurice Bamford picked the right man to lead 'Fax to resurrection from the dead in 1978.

Things could not have been worse when Mick arrived at Thrum Hall just before the Challenge Cup transfer deadline in February 1978. Halifax were bottom of the league, had lost all twenty of their league fixtures and been knocked out of the Yorkshire Cup, the Players Trophy and the Floodlit Trophy without making any progress through the rounds. The average league crowd at Thrum Hall had plummeted to 1,341. A messianic figure was needed. It is arguable who was more important in the revival – Bamford or Blacker? Both were gifts from God, as far as Halifax were concerned. Mick cost 'Fax £1,000 and former skipper Lee Greenwood also went to Odsal as part of the deal.

Barnsley-born Mick had learned his rugby in Huddersfield and had been signed from Birkby Youth Club by Bradford Northern. Mick had put in over a decade of loyal service at Odsal and been rewarded with a record testimonial of £4,020 in 1977. Everyone knew Mick as a model player, who never gave less than his best and who could play anywhere in the backs and had even turned out at loose forward, despite his lack of stature – height-wise, at least. Mick was only 5' 6" tall but in

his later years, he seemed to be that wide too!

He had made 202 appearances for Northern, scoring 47 tries since his debut in 1967. He had been a member of Northern's 'A' team which had won the Yorkshire Senior Competition Challenge Cup in 1970/71, had played at Wembley in defeat against Featherstone Rovers in 1973 and had been stand-off when Bradford beat Widnes 3-2 at Wilderspool in the John Player Trophy final in 1975. In 1972 he had been capped by Yorkshire, when they beat Lancashire 32-18 at Castleford. That was his only representative recognition at senior level, perhaps not surprisingly, given the opposition for stand-off honours from the likes of Roger Millward, Dave Topliss and Mick Shoebottom, to name three Yorkshire rivals.

Bamford immediately made Mick club captain, a position he held for three years, while he was also player-coach for two. Mick set an example that others could not ignore. He tackled like a demon, ran courageously at the biggest of opponents and massed defences, prised openings for others, rallied his men when they were flagging, cajoled them into giving more then they thought they had and fused the team into one in which the fans could once more take pride. Mick never

*The Halifax team which Mick Blacker led against Leeds in the 1979 Yorkshire Cup final. From left to right, back row: Mick Snee, Maurice Bamford (coach), Peter Jarvis, Jimmy Birts, Graham Garrod, Greg Sharpe, Mick Scott, Dave Busfield, Dave Callon. Front row: Derek Howard, Dave Cholmondeley, Terry Langton, Mick Blacker, Dean Raistrick, Keith Waites, Alan Wood.*

seemed to give up and neither did his team.

From the start Mick led by example. In his first seven games he played stand-off, scrum-half, loose forward and left-centre, as the new team began to form. In those seven games Halifax finally won twice – 13-5 at Huyton and 10-7 at Thrum Hall against Batley. Halifax still finished bottom but everyone knew that they were now upwardly mobile.

The 1978/79 season was a triumph for Mick and his men. Promotion was only just missed, the average crowd went up by almost 1,000 and Halifax knocked out First Division Castleford on their way to the Yorkshire Cup semi-final, in which they were unlucky to lose 2-4 to York. Mick won the Player of the Season award and led the try-scorers with 13 in 32 matches, all at stand-off. Mick's half-back partnership with Terry Langton was at the core of Halifax's revival.

The 1979/80 season was even better. Halifax won promotion as Mick led a side that pulled together and proved the old adage that the sum of certain teams is greater than the quality of the individuals. Halifax performed wonders by reaching the Yorkshire Cup final, putting out Bramley, Hunslet and Dewsbury before falling 6-15 to Leeds in the final – iniquitously, in those days, held at

Headingley, despite Leeds qualifying. There was more excitement in the Challenge Cup. Halifax negotiated three difficult ties, at Barrow, Featherstone Rovers and at home to Wakefield Trinity. Mick missed the latter having suffered a ruptured appendix. However, he recovered to play in the semi-final against Hull KR at Leeds only to suffer a shoulder injury in a 7-20 defeat.

Halifax made a brave attempt to retain their Division One status in 1980/81 but just did not have the resources. They were unlucky to go down, winning eleven of their thirty games. Mick led them to a 3-2 victory over Wigan in the Cup and the third round of the John Player trophy was reached.

The next season Halifax won promotion again. Jimmy Birts had gone to Wigan and Mick took over at full-back, playing 25 of his 31 games there. His final season at Thrum Hall, 1982/83, was an anti-climax. Halifax did not invest in players and in May 1982 Mick and his co-coach Ken Loxton resigned, although Mick remained as a player until transferred to Warrington. He later moved to Mansfield Marksman. In later years Mick coached amateurs at Greetland All Rounders, Park Amateurs and Halifax Irish. He was one of those players the fans never forget.

# Steve Bond

Loose forward, second-row forward, 1981-1986

**Previous club:** Bramley

**Halifax debut:** 30 August 1981 v. Batley

**Final Halifax appearance:** 18 May 1986
v. Warrington Premiership final

**Appearances:** 134 + 19 subs

**Tries:** 26  **Goals:** 3 drop goals  **Points:** 91

**Transferred to:** Bradford Northern

Twenty-six year-old Steve Bond had a lot to live up to when he signed for Halifax in 1981. He had cost Halifax a club-record fee of £20,000, although Bramley had originally listed him at £35,000. Moreover, he was effectively the replacement for the popular and talented Mick Scott, who had just moved on to Wigan. Steve remained a Thrum Haller for five years and certainly came up to scratch.

Castleford-born, Steve had trials for Dewsbury but was signed eventually by Bramley, making his debut in a 14-14 draw at York on 11 January 1976. Among his first teammates were Peter Goodchild, Keith Waites and Terry Dewhirst. Steve helped Bramley to promotion in 1976/77, when Neil Fox was used at second row with Steve at loose forward. In five years at McLaren Field Steve made almost 150 appearances (22 tries, 2 drop goals) and was coveted by many more fashionable clubs.

At Thrum Hall he proved durable, industrious and sometimes inspirational. Steve played well above his weight, ran hard and often and was a dreadnought defender. He also had that little bit of extra class which enabled him to make the improbable break, slip the unexpected pass or drop the occasional goal.

It was a drop goal against Hunslet in a tense 17-15 victory at Thrum Hall which gave him his first score for the club on 27 September 1981, while his first try followed a fortnight later in a 31-21 success at Cardiff City Blue Dragons. His first season saw him top the appearances chart with 35 and his return of 12 tries was a career best. His consistent displays

earned him the Player of the Year award, after a season which ended in promotion from fourth spot in Division Two.

A disastrous season in the First Division followed but Steve battled away, playing in 30 matches, the highlight of his campaign being two match-clinching tries in a 13-5 first round Challenge Cup victory at Huddersfield. Promotion in 1983/84 took Halifax back up with Steve moving into the second-row, usually with Alan Shillito, to accommodate Terry Langton at loose forward.

Steve had a fine season in the First Division in 1984/85, when, despite the massive influx of Australians, he once more topped the appearances list with 36. He figured in many games at second row again as Paul Langmack filled the number thirteen jersey so well. For the first time he came close to appearing in a major final only for Halifax to lose to Hull KR in the Players Trophy semi-final.

In 1985/86 he finally did appear in a final when Halifax lost to Warrington in the Premiership final at Elland Road, substituting for Neil James in the twenty-ninth minute. Coincidentally, it was his last game for 'Fax. He had already, of course, picked up a Championship-winners' medal, appearing in 18 of Halifax's 30 league fixtures.

# John Burnett

Right-centre, 1954-1967

**Previous club:** Pellon ARL

**Halifax debut:** 16 January 1954 v. Dewsbury

**Final Halifax appearance:** 15 April 1967
v. Workington Town

**Appearances:** 340 + 4 subs

**Tries:** 130   **Goals:** 0   **Points:** 390

**Transferred to:** Bradford Northern

**Honours:** Yorkshire

John Burnett shares with George Kitson (1902/03), Joe Riley (1906/07) and Chris Anderson (1985/86) the distinction of captaining a Halifax side to the Championship. That is very select company indeed and John ranks high in the pantheon of great players to have represented the club. Like Kitson (born in Halifax) and Riley (born in Sowerby Bridge), John was a local. He was born and bred in Pellon and cost Halifax the princely sum of £200 when he was signed in 1953, aged seventeen.

His record of 344 first-team appearances and 130 tries between 1954 and 1967 indicates tellingly just how good a bargain Halifax got. It was obvious that John would become a fine centre but his immediate prospects were limited as Halifax's great team of the 1950s was not an easy XIII to break into. His debut at left-centre alongside Tommy Lynch saw John score an interception try after only three minutes against Dewsbury in a 14-0 win at Thrum Hall. He would have to wait over three years before his next appearance in the first team. National service

in the RAF prevented him from making much headway beyond outings for the 'A' team, although he did have a loan spell at Blackpool Borough in September-October 1955, when he played 6 games, including an exciting 24-24 draw with the New Zealanders – only his second first-class game.

John finally established himself at right-centre shortly after the start of the 1957/58 season, striking up a memorable partnership with Geoff Palmer, which would cause other sides big problems for the next four years. John's right-flank partnership with Alan Snowden was another powerful weapon in Halifax's armoury over the same period. John scored 19 tries in 33 outings in 1957/58, when Halifax won the Yorkshire League.

At this stage in his career John was a very quick, direct player. The following years saw him develop into a brainy, creative centre, who could utilise his winger to great advantage. Defensively, John left little to be desired, while physically, at 6' and over fourteen stones, he was a match for anyone in an era when good, big centres were a prime requisite.

In 1958/59 Halifax slipped to twelfth in the table but John enjoyed a fine season personally. He scored his first hat-trick in a 34-6 home win against Bramley and finished with 27 tries in 37 games, the best return of his career. He also partnered Alan Snowden in two Roses Matches – a 35-19 victory at Craven Park, Hull and a 16-15 success in the play-off for the County Championship at

Leigh. Jack Wilkinson also shared those triumphs. John and Alan again played in combination for Yorkshire against Cumberland and Lancashire the following season, while John added to his tally of caps by playing in both games in 1960/61.

The 1959/60 season saw Halifax drop even further to twenty-second in the league but John still ran in 19 tries in 38 matches, played in his first Yorkshire Cup semi-final and appeared against the Australians. The 1960/61 season brought an appearance against the 1960 New Zealand World Cup team and a Challenge Cup semi-final defeat by Wigan, the nearest he ever got to Wembley. 1961/62 brought John his first taste of the club captaincy and he led his team to a place in the newly formed First Division in 1962/63. Alan Marchant took over the leadership for 1962/63 and 1963/64. In the former campaign John had his first experience of playing in the pack, twice filling the loose-forward jersey.

By then John had developed a constructive partnership with Duncan Jackson, a speedy and resourceful right-winger. John played in both the Yorkshire Cup final and Eastern Division Championship final victories of 1963/64, his winger scoring in both games. He received a club record £1,000 benefit in 1964.

John's greatest success came in the following season, however, when he took over the captaincy from Ken Roberts in January 1965. His leadership played a big role in Halifax's scintillating run to the Championship final and his own form was wonderful. He regained his scoring touch, finishing the season with 21 tries, more than any other centre in the league, while Jackson bagged another 20. In the Championship play-offs John scored tries against Leeds at Thrum Hall and in the semi-final at Castleford, while in an outstanding display against St Helens in the final at Swinton he scored twice at crucial stages. In addition to the Championship, Halifax won the Mackeson Trophy as the game's most prolific scorers and were runners-up in the Yorkshire League. John had passed a personal landmark on 10 October 1964, in a 27-7 home defeat of Leeds, when he scored his 100th try for Halifax.

In 1965/66 John and his team performed wonders to again qualify for the Championship final from tenth position in the league. They were simply brilliant in the play-offs, winning seemingly impossible games at Bradford Northern, Swinton and Wigan before falling heavily to St Helens in the final.

John's last season, 1966/67, at Thrum Hall was less successful, although he did lead his team to the semi-finals of the Yorkshire Cup before giving up the captaincy on 1 December 1966. The great team was disintegrating and John found himself playing loose forward, second row and once even at prop. It was then that he gave ample evidence that he might have made a splendid ball-playing forward. Perhaps appropriately, though, he finished the campaign with seven appearances in the familiar number three jersey, partnering the newly-signed Peter Goodchild.

In recent years John has returned to the club as a valuable administrator and fund-raiser. But his name will always be associated with those momentous days of the 1960s.

**Previous club:** Sandal RU

**Halifax debut:** 14 December 1969 v. York

**Final Halifax appearance:** 11 January 1976
    v. Huyton

**Appearances:** 170 + 13 subs

**Tries:** 77    **Goals:** 348 + 1 drop goal

**Points:** 928

**Transferred to:** Castleford

**Honours:** Yorkshire, Great Britain Under-24s

Son of the former Wakefield Trinity forward Harry Burton, Bruce was captured from rugby union for a signing fee of £1,000, a large amount for an untried teenager. In the event Bruce Burton was an inspired acquisition. He was a player of class, versatile, extremely quick and nimble, and he could score tries from any part of the field, some of them extraordinary. In addition he was Halifax's first regular round-the-corner goal-kicker, although Barrie Cooper had previously employed that style in his brief career at Thrum Hall.

Although signing in 1969, Bruce did not become Halifax's first choice stand-off until the 1971/72 season. In 1970/71 he proved successful as a winger and occasionally as full-back, when Alan Kellett rejoined the club and took over at number six. The 1971/72 campaign catapulted Bruce to fame. He was a key member of the side which won the inaugural John Player trophy. His performance in the final, when he landed five goals, earned him the Man of the Match award and alerted the rugby league world to his huge talent. He finished the season with 159 points, the first of five consecutive seasons in which he would top 150.

On 27 August 1972 he re-wrote the Halifax record book, when he claimed 31 points (14 goals, 1 try) in a 76-8 massacre of Hunslet at Parkside in a first round Yorkshire Cup-tie. No one has since matched his goals tally and only John Schuster, in 1994, has surpassed his 31-points mark. Burton frequently scored all his side's points and was an out and out match-winner. In the 1973/74 season, when Halifax won promotion, he played in all 35 of Halifax's fixtures piling up 241 points. At Huyton he scored 24 points (4 tries, 6 goals) and against Doncaster at Thrum Hall he bagged 23 points (3 tries, 7 goals). Not included in official records were the 26 points (4 tries, 7 goals) he gathered against Huddersfield in the annual Charity Cup.

In 1974/75 he won three caps for Yorkshire, playing stand-off and centre. Halifax made Burton captain for the 1975/76 season. His form was as good as ever in a disappointing campaign, which ended in relegation. Bruce was Halifax's main asset and far too good for Second Division rugby. Bradford offered a massive £9,000 for him but the terms were unsatisfactory to Halifax and he was sold to Castleford for £6,000 (plus Gary Brook), worthily succeeding the great Alan Hardisty.

His potential was realised at Castleford and he captained Great Britain Under-24s in their two victories over France in 1976. In 1977 he scored two fantastic tries and a drop goal to win the White Rose Trophy in Castleford's 17-7 Yorkshire Cup final success against Featherstone. Sadly, injury ended his career prematurely in 1980.

# Dave Callon
Prop, second-row forward, 1971-1982

**Previous club:** Normanton ARL

**Halifax debut:** 24 February 1971 v. Oldham

**Final Halifax appearance:** 29 August 1982
v. Barrow

**Appearances:** 188 + 44 subs

**Tries:** 23    **Goals:** 0    **Points:** 69

**Transferred to:** Retired

Many wonderful forwards have worn Halifax's famous blue and white hoops but few have been steadier or more loyal than Dave Callon, or have cost less, for his signing-on fee in November 1970 was a mere £100. For that Halifax got a dozen years of service – 232 appearances at less than ten bob (50p) each. Dave was twenty when he arrived at Thrum Hall and had played for a successful Normanton side, which had won the Yorkshire Cup at Under-17 and Under-19 levels.

In his prime Dave stood a shade over six feet tall and weighed 14st 7lb. Although not a flashy player, he was a fine all-round forward, who worked hard in defence and was resolute in taking the ball forward. He was always liable to make the half-break and judicious in passing to better-placed colleagues. He was unselfish and developed a speciality in taking passes one-handed, yet hardly ever spilled the ball. Dave was certainly a good team player, who did all that was expected when the going got tough but still managed to play a disciplined game.

Dave made his first-team debut as a seventieth-minute substitute for Terry Dewhirst in a 7-29 defeat at Watersheddings three months after his signing and played the rest of his first season in the reserves. The following season was a completely different story, as he broke into the first team and clocked up 42 appearances. After starting in the second row, he settled at blind-side prop and was one of the surprises as Halifax stormed to the final of the John Player Trophy. That game at Odsal was his twenty-

sixth as a professional. Halifax beat hot favourites Wakefield Trinity 22-11 and Dave scored the final try – his first for the club.

An equally vital try in less exalted surroundings followed in the first round of the cup at Huyton, giving Halifax a 7-4 victory and paving the way for a surge to the semi-final, when Halifax lost to Leeds.

Halifax won promotion in 1973/74 but Dave was injured on 27 January 1974 and did not play for another three years, not because of the injury but through his work commitments. He returned in dire times – his fifth game back was the notorious low-water mark of the Cawoods disaster. Things improved, however, and Dave blossomed into an outstanding performer, mostly in the second-row, in one of Halifax's most popular teams. In 1979/80 he was in the side which contested the Yorkshire Cup final, reached the Challenge Cup semi-final and won promotion. He was also a member of the team which was promoted in 1981/82 and few who saw them will forget his part in the marvellous set moves with Ken Loxton and Mick Scott, which so often resulted in tries. Just before he retired he was rewarded with a benefit of almost £4,500.

# Dennis Chalkley
Full-back, 1946-1952

**Previous club:** Sharlston ARL

**Halifax debut:** 23 April 1946 v. Workington Town

**Final Halifax appearance:** 22 November 1952 v. Keighley

**Appearances:** 146

**Tries:** 4    **Goals:** 248    **Points:** 508

**Transferred to:** Hull Kingston Rovers

Dennis Chalkley was a full-back of the old school – a steady defender, reliable, with good powers of anticipation and positioning. He was an accomplished goal-kicker and a field-kicker of considerable range and he very nearly did not play for Halifax.

On Good Friday, 19 April 1946 Dennis played full-back for Leeds, who lost 10-12 to Halifax at Headingley. Leeds did not sign him but Halifax did and on the following Tuesday he turned out for Halifax in a 22-18 win over Workington Town at Thrum Hall. Dennis took over the full-back position from the legendary Hubert Lockwood, against whom he had played at Leeds. Hubert was a hard act to follow and it took a while before Dennis could call the number one jersey his own.

Dennis came from Sharlston, and was nineteen when he joined Halifax. He landed his first goal of 248 in a 17-3 home victory over Castleford on 27 April 1946. In his first full season, 1946/47, he shared the full-back role with Friend Taylor, both players making 20 appearances and landing 24 goals.

In 1948/49 Halifax brought Ron Durston from Wales to fill the full-back position but Dennis displaced him. He kicked a goal in Halifax's 8-10 loss to the Australians and hit a

rich vein of form in the second half of the season, as Halifax confounded everyone by reaching Wembley. Dennis's kicking played a significant part in Halifax's success, crucial goals in the first round against Hull and the third round at Oldham helping to carry Halifax to the semi-final. In the semi against Huddersfield at Odsal Dennis landed four goals, including an ice-cool conversion of Stan Kielty's try, which gave the Thrum Hallers a sensational 11-10 victory.

At Wembley, before a world-record crowd of 95,050, Dennis was one of Halifax's better performers in a disappointing final, which saw Bradford Northern win 12-0. Dennis never even got a shot at goal, so complete was Bradford's dominance, despite the low score.

In 1949/50 Dennis was ever-present in Halifax's 42 games, landing 90 goals and failing to score only four times. His best haul was six against Wakefield Trinity. Halifax reached the Championship semi-finals, Dennis kicking a goal in a 5-5 draw at Wigan and another in the replay, only for 'Fax to lose 2-18. He played in two unusual fixtures at Thrum Hall, kicking five goals in a 28-13 victory over Bordeaux and two in a 33-6 beating of Ystradgynlais.

In 1950/51 Dennis added another 59 goals in 31 appearances, and passed the 200 mark with four successes in a home first-round Challenge Cup-tie against Hunslet. His last two seasons produced only 20 appearances (37 goals) as competition for the full-back position from Gwylim Bowen and Tuss Griffiths led to his departure from the club.

# David Cholmondeley
### Centre, 1978-1982

**Previous club:** Dudley Hill ARL

**Halifax debut:** 27 March 1978 v. Swinton

**Final Halifax appearance:** 7 May 1982
    v. Doncaster

**Appearances:** 136 + 2 subs

**Tries:** 22   **Goals:** 24   **Points:** 114

**Transferred to:** Bramley

Hunslet-born Dave ('Chum') Cholmondeley joined Halifax in March 1978, towards the close of the worst season, bar possibly that of 2003, in the club's history. He signed for £600 and was a product of the Dudley Hill club, from where Halifax, within a few days, also obtained stand-off Albert Hannah and prop forward Steve Laws.

Dave went straight into the first team and remained there until he left four years later. A model of consistency, Dave missed only eight games of the 146 which the Thrum Hallers contested in that period, in which Halifax regained much of the pride and respect they had lost in the preceding years. Dave was a solidly built (5' 10" and 13st) twenty-three-year-old centre when he joined 'Fax and he developed into a very sound all-round performer, who defended extremely well, took the right options in attack and could produce a good burst of speed. He could also kick goals, when the first-choice kicker was missing or struggling.

During his debut season it took Halifax until 11 April 1978 before they won a game at Thrum Hall – Dave's third game. He landed two goals, including a conversion of Dave Callon's last-minute try, in a 10-7 victory over Batley. Anyone would have thought they had won the Challenge Cup when the goal went over and the referee blew for time.

Matters improved rapidly. From rock bottom in 1977/78 Halifax almost won promotion in 1978/79 and were just edged out of the Yorkshire Cup by York, who beat them 4-2 in the semi-final at Thrum Hall. Dave started the season on the left wing but settled at left-centre, which became his accustomed position from then on.

In 1979/80 Halifax won promotion, Dave missing just one of the 36 games played. The Yorkshire Cup final was also reached, 'Fax losing to Leeds at Headingley. Dave played in all the rounds, scoring twice against Hunslet in a 23-12 second round victory. He was also an ever-present in the ties which took Halifax to the Challenge Cup semi-final and another Headingley defeat, this time to Hull KR. During the season Dave played full-back in a league fixture at Featherstone, the only occasion he ever wore the number one jersey for Halifax.

Halifax were unlucky to be relegated in 1980/81, when Dave scored 40 points (6 tries, 11 goals) in 34 appearances. He landed four goals in a 17-9 win at Leigh and four goals and a try in a 23-19 home victory over Salford – his best scoring returns for Halifax.

Dave helped Halifax to promotion in 1981/82, his last season at Thrum Hall. In 34 appearances he contributed 9 goals and 5 tries. In his last game for Halifax, a 32-5 home win against Doncaster, he landed two goals. He was transferred to Bramley in exchange for hooker Russell Sowden, following 'Fax stalwarts Tony Garforth and Kenny Loxton.

# Des Clarkson

Loose forward, 1951-1954

**Previous club:** Leeds

**Halifax debut:** 1 December 1951 v. Batley

**Final Halifax appearance:** 18 September 1954 v. Leeds

**Appearances:** 116

**Tries:** 22   **Goals:** 89   **Points:** 244

**Transferred to:** Keighley

**Honours:** Yorkshire, England, Tour Trialist (1946)

By the time Des Clarkson joined Halifax he was twenty-eight and had amassed a wealth of experience with Hunslet, Leigh and Leeds, as well as earning county and international caps. Born in Castleford and a miner by trade, Des had been the subject of a £2,000 transfer fee on his moves from Hunslet to Leigh and again from Leigh to Leeds, which was big money at that period. Halifax got him for £1,250 and he proved to be the last part in the formation of Halifax's great pack of the 1950s.

Fair-haired and robust (6' 1" and 15st 7lbs), Des was a cool, constructive and hard-working loose forward who fitted in excellently with the Halifax half-backs Ken Dean and Stan Kielty. He certainly solved Halifax's loose forward problem. The club had tried Albert Fearnley there but he was a more natural second-rower, and Jack Wilkinson had been drafted in, but everyone knew 'Wilkie' was more suited to the front row, while Frank Birkin, potentially a great loose forward, was too ill-disciplined.

Although Des's career at Thrum Hall lasted less than three years he packed a lot in. Not only was he an outstanding number fourteen (like most Yorkshire clubs, Halifax did not use a number thirteen jersey), but he was also a reliable goal-kicker, who landed almost 400

goals in his rugby league career, which stretched over more than 400 games.

In 1952/53 he picked up a Yorkshire League winners' medal and played in the Championship final, when Halifax lost 14-24 to St Helens at Maine Road. He shared with Stan Kielty the achievement of playing in 47 of Halifax's 48 fixtures, scoring 9 tries and 49 goals, twice landing six in a match and thrice kicking five. The following season he played 41 games, figuring in all Halifax's titanic games with Warrington at Wembley, Odsal and Maine Road. In the drawn Challenge Cup final he was one of the best performers. Jim Sullivan wrote, 'Desmond Clarkson was the best forward on the field for me. He was the main inspiration for the Yorkshiremen.'

Unfortunately, Des only picked up runners-up medals for the cup and Championship but at least he had finally played at Wembley, having previously suffered defeats in semi-finals with both Hunslet and Leeds. The 1953/54 season did, however, provide him with a second successive Yorkshire League winners' medal, making his tally three for the competition, having been with Leeds when they won it in 1950/51.

Des later played for Keighley and Castleford, becoming 'A' team coach at Wheldon Road. Des was one of few players to have made over 100 appearances for three clubs – Hunslet, for whom his father had also played, Leeds and Halifax. Des died on 16 January 2002.

# Mike Condon
Open-side prop, 1948-1953

**Previous club:** Swansea RU

**Halifax debut:** 11 December 1948 v.
Liverpool Stanley

**Final Halifax appearance:** 12 December 1953
v. York

**Appearances:** 146

**Tries:** 4   **Goals:** 0   **Points:** 12

**Transferred to:** Retired

**Honours:** Wales

When a scribe wrote 'Condon is the hero of many battles' prior to the Championship final of 1953, he was right in two senses. Mike Condon had been decorated for valour while serving with the South Wales Borderers in the Second World War, as well as figuring heroically in plenty of hard-fought rugby matches, both union and league.

Mike came very late to rugby league. The Swansea prop forward was twenty-nine when he joined Halifax in return for a £450 signing fee in December 1948. The odds on his succeeding were pretty long but he exceeded all expectations. A great scrummager and tireless forager, Mike was fair-haired and boulder-shaped at only 5' 8" and fifteen stones. He took some shifting.

Halifax assembled a rag, tag and bobtail team in 1948/49, which finished twenty-fifth in the league but miraculously fought its way to a Wembley Challenge Cup final. One of the key factors was the strength of the front row, composed of Mike, Alvin Ackerley and Jack Rothwell. The trio were ball-winners supreme during that great cup run, which saw Hull, Swinton, Oldham and Huddersfield beaten. Surprisingly, however, they were walloped for possession in the final, as 'Fax went down 0-12 to Bradford Northern before a world-record crowd of 95,050.

Halifax rose to fourth in 1949/50 but Mike lost his place to the giant Don Hatfield and to fellow Welshman Len Olsen, playing only 9 matches but scoring his first try

for the Thrum Hallers in a 24-10 home victory over Rochdale Hornets.

He was back in favour in 1950/51, playing 33 games. The following season he added 37 appearances and was in the team which defeated the New Zealanders 18-12 at Thrum Hall. It was the 1952/53 season, however, which brought him most pleasure. He played 40 games for Halifax, who finished second in the league and won the Yorkshire League Championship. He appeared in Halifax's fixture against the Australians and in their Yorkshire Cup semi-final loss to Huddersfield after a replay. Amazingly, by the close of the season Halifax had four Welsh props vying for two places – Mike, Len Olsen, Bryn Hopkins and John Thorley. Mike and Jack Wilkinson were the choices when it came to the Championship final clash with St Helens at Maine Road, which ended in a 14-24 defeat.

The Championship final more or less ended Mike's first team career – he would only add two more appearances – but he carried on playing for the hugely successful 'A' team for a couple of years.

The war probably prevented Mike from winning union honours but he won 3 caps for Wales at rugby league. In 1952 he played in defeats by France at Bordeaux and by England at Wigan but was a winner against Other Nationalities at Warrington in 1953.

# Terry Cook
Left-winger, 1950-1953

**Previous club:** Cardiff RU

**Halifax debut:** 26 August 1950 v. Leigh

**Final Halifax appearance:** 9 May 1953 v. St Helens Championship final

**Appearances:** 102

**Tries:** 48   **Goals:** 0   **Points:** 144

**Transferred to:** Retired

**Honours:** Wales, Great Britain (non-test)

Terry Cook was a dual Welsh International, whose senior career in rugby union lasted just about as long as his career in rugby league – three years. He packed a lot into both.

Born in 1927, he made his initial impact with Pontypool, playing as a twenty-year-old for a combined Pontypool-Blaenavon-Talywain XV against the 1947 Wallabies. Among his teammates were future league men in Don Gullick, Ray Cale and Don Hayward. He moved to Cardiff in 1948, scoring 44 tries in 71 appearances. He won caps for Wales against Scotland and Ireland in 1949, playing alongside legendary three-quarters, Ken Jones, Jack Matthews and Bleddyn Williams.

Halifax persuaded him to come north, signing him on 12 August 1950 for £2,000 on a three-year contract. Curly haired Terry, 5' 10.5" and 12st 10lbs, was a real handful for opposing wingmen – quick, strong-running and dangerous – while he was also a hefty tackler. Halifax were in a period of transition when Terry came to Thrum Hall, not yet the force they would become by the time he left.

A try-scoring debut on the left wing in a 5-13 home loss to Leigh was a good start. His first season brought him 19 tries in 31 games, only right-winger Arthur Daniels scoring more. Included were home and away hat-tricks against Castleford. Terry certainly

found his feet quickly, for on 31 March 1951 he was capped by Wales, scoring twice against Brian Bevan at Swansea, in a game won 27-21 by the Other Nationalities. A fortnight later he scored again in a 13-28 defeat by France in Marseilles. On 19 May 1951 he represented Great Britain against Australasia at Headingley in a game celebrating the Festival of Britain.

In 1951/52 Terry registered 15 tries in 38 games for Halifax, including more hat-tricks against Batley and Liverpool City. He played in Halifax's 18-12 success against the New Zealanders and won his third Welsh cap against Other Nationalities at Abertillery. The following season was Terry's swansong. Halifax won the Yorkshire League, were beaten semi-finalists in the Yorkshire Cup and finished second in the league. Terry contributed 14 tries in 33 appearances. He was Halifax's sole try-scorer in a torrid encounter with the Australians, which was lost 7-39, while one of his most crucial tries, and his last in first-class rugby, helped pull Halifax through 18-16 against Bradford Northern in the Championship semi-final at Thrum Hall. A couple of weeks earlier he had won his fourth Welsh cap in an 18-16 victory over Other Nationalities at Warrington.

Terry played for Halifax in the 1953 Championship final against St Helens, his last first-class game, but had to settle for a losers' medal as Saints, with his old Pontypool mates Ray Cale and Don Gullick in the side, triumphed 24-14.

# Paul Daley
Scrum-half, 1962-1968

**Previous club:** Featherstone Intermediates ARL

**Halifax debut:** 27 October 1962 v. Wigan

**Final Halifax appearance:** 26 January 1968 v. Featherstone Rovers

**Appearances:** 104 + 4 subs

**Tries:** 49  **Goals:** 1  **Points:** 149

**Transferred to:** Bradford Northern

Paul Daley signed for Halifax in October 1962 for £300 and made his first-team debut within weeks in a stunning 33-10 rout of Wigan at Thrum Hall. The tenure of club skipper Alan Marchant was immediately under threat but it was two years before Paul finally made the Halifax number seven jersey his. In the meantime, the Featherstone-born scrum-half dazzled in the 'A' team, forming a half-back partnership with Dave Stockwell that many thought would eventually be as good as that of Ken Dean and Stan Kielty.

In 1962/63 Paul won the 'A' team Player of the Year award and the following year ran in 20 tries in 25 appearances for the Reserves, who won the Yorkshire Senior Competition Shield at a canter. Paul also played 9 first-team games, including 4 in the Eastern Division Championship, which Halifax won.

The 1964/65 season saw him installed as first-choice scrum-half, following Marchant's transfer to Hunslet. It is doubtful if Halifax have ever had a quicker scrum-half than the lightweight, whizz-bang Daley, who was a real flier off the mark and capable of scoring some virtuoso tries. He and Barry Robinson must have been the best pair of supporting half-backs the club ever possessed, always backing up breaks by their colleagues. Paul scored 19 tries in 1964/65, breaking Herbert Fletcher's club record of 17 for a half-back, set in 1929/30, and played a big part in Halifax's drive to the Rugby League Championship. In the play-offs running up to the final he scored five tries – two each against Leeds and Featherstone Rovers at Thrum Hall and one

in the epic 26-18 semi-final victory at Castleford, the latter one of the most crucial and spectacular in the club's history.

He was not so lucky the following season. After scoring 17 tries in 34 games, Paul broke his ankle in a 30-2 victory at Batley and missed the last seven games of the season, including Halifax's second consecutive Championship final against St Helens.

His career at Thrum Hall petered out over the next couple of years, although he did play in a Yorkshire Cup semi-final against Featherstone Rovers in the 1966/67 season, when he also scored his second hat-trick for Halifax in a home game against York.

In 1968 a £2,000 transfer took Paul to Bradford Northern, for whom he scored 9 tries in 56 appearances. From Odsal he moved to Hull Kingston Rovers, where in 1971, partnering Roger Millward, he earned a Yorkshire Cup-winners' medal, when Rovers beat Castleford 11-7 in the final at Wakefield. At Craven Park, Paul appeared in a further 59 games for the Robins, claiming 7 tries and a solitary goal.

After retiring from playing Paul went on to considerable coaching success with Hunslet, for whom he also played a few games, Batley, York and Featherstone Rovers.

# Arthur Daniels

Right-winger, 1945-1957

**Previous club:** Llanelli RU

**Halifax debut:** 25 August 1945 v. Swinton

**Final Halifax appearance:** 22 April 1957 v. Hull

**Appearances:** 377

**Tries:** 216   **Goals:** 3   **Points:** 654

**Transferred to:** Bradford Northern

**Honours:** Wales, Great Britain

When Arthur Daniels scored the first of two tries in a 32-11 home win against Bramley on 17 March 1956, he became the first Halifax player to score 200 tries for the club. It was a fantastic achievement for a player, who, in the early stages of his career, many critics had deemed too slow to make a first-class rugby league winger. However, Arthur, who had always been a competent defensive wingman, became arguably the finest all-round winger to have represented Halifax.

Arthur Harper Daniels hailed from Pontyberem, a small mining village in South Wales, and was happy to leave the pit when 'Fax enticed him north aged twenty-one in 1945. He had played union for Pontyberem and Llanelli. Fellow Llanelli players, full-back John Davies and hooker Bill Pritchard, came to Thrum Hall at the same time. Arthur scored his first try for the club in his first league match, a 31-3 home win against Swinton but, playing in a mediocre side, had totalled only 8 tries in 30 games by the close of the season. Call-up to the Services restricted him to a single appearance in 1946/47 but he was back in harness from October 1947, when one of his first appearances was against the Kiwis, who beat Halifax 21-5.

The 1948/49 season brought Arthur into the limelight. Sturdily built (5' 10" and 12st

7lbs) and always sporting a centre parting to his hair, Arthur had become a popular figure on 'Fax's right wing. He had worked hard at his game and had sharpened up his pace. The extra speed, allied to his fitness, elusiveness, determination, exemplary tackling and natural footballing ability, made him a very dangerous wingman and he was rewarded with his first cap for Wales on 5 February 1949, when he was a try-scorer in a 14-10 defeat of England at Swansea. He went on to score a record 9 tries for Wales in 13 internationals. Halifax too enjoyed unexpected success in battling their way through to the Challenge Cup final, despite finishing near the bottom of the league. Arthur played in every round, scoring vital tries in the first three – at home against Hull (won 10-0 in the second leg) and Swinton (5-0) and away at Oldham (7-2). He got little chance to shine at Wembley, however, where Bradford Northern won 12-0.

The 1948/49 campaign had seen Arthur top the club's try-scorers for the first time. He claimed 18 in 41 games, including his first hat-tricks against Hull KR and York, while he had also made his first appearance against the Australians, who won 10-8 at Thrum Hall on 27 November 1948.

Arthur performed brilliantly in 1949/50, helping Halifax to reach the top four play-offs. In 37 games he rattled up 34 tries. Included were four in a 28-3 victory over Whitehaven and hat-tricks against Dewsbury, Hunslet and Batley. He was arguably the best British right-wingman in the game and was selected for the

*Arthur Daniels slips over for one of his double-century of tries for 'Fax. Stan Kielty is in support on the left.*

Lions tour in 1950. Unfortunately for Arthur injuries wrecked his tour. A leg injury kept him out of the First Test and then a broken collarbone virtually ended his participation. He played 5 tour games, scoring 5 tries before returning home early from New Zealand.

Twenty-one tries in 32 appearances for Halifax in 1950/51 made him leading try-scorer again and indicated that his injuries had not seriously affected him. The following season brought him 28 tries in 39 games. He was a scorer in Halifax's 18-12 win over the New Zealanders and bagged four in a 26-9 home victory against Widnes. More significant, however, was the birth of his partnership with centre Tommy Lynch. The two were first paired together on New Year's Day 1952 in an 18-5 beating of Rochdale Hornets at Thrum Hall. For the next four years Daniels and Lynch became synonymous with the very best of wing-centre play, delighting Halifax fans with their clever manoeuvres and deceptions and piling up 185 tries between them in 142 games as partners.

Arthur was made captain for the 1952/53 season, which began well for him but ended tragically. He was in such good form that he played in the first two Ashes Tests, scoring a try in the first at Headingley (won 19-6). A splintered ankle bone sustained in the second test at Swinton (won 21-5) kept him out of the third. Christmas Day 1952 provided him with a try and a broken arm in Halifax's 6-12 home loss to Huddersfield and ended his season. Halifax won the Yorkshire League, providing Arthur with his first winners' medal, and were runners-up to St Helens in the Championship.

In 1953/54 Arthur won his second Yorkshire League Championship medal and played in Halifax's momentous trilogy against Warrington at Wembley, Odsal and Maine Road, picking up runners-up medals for the Challenge Cup and Championship. His disallowed try at Odsal late in the game was a major point of disputation for years. Arthur contributed 27 tries in 45 appearances in 1953/54. The following season he ran over for 25 in 38 games and he was a member of the team which beat Hull 22-14 in the Yorkshire Cup final, scoring a second-half try.

1955/56 was Halifax's last as a major power in this period and Arthur was as deadly as ever. He equalled his own post-war record with 34 tries in 46 matches. One of his touchdowns won the Yorkshire Cup for Halifax, who beat Hull 7-0 in the final, a replay, to retain the trophy. He also earned his third Yorkshire League winners' medal but had to again settle for runners-up medals as Halifax lost to St Helens at Wembley and to Hull in the Championship final.

**Previous club:** Normanton ARL

**Halifax debut:** 17 October 1969 v. Hunslet

**Final Halifax appearance:** 27 August 1978 v. Castleford Yorkshire Cup

**Appearances:** 208 + 22 subs

**Tries:** 38    **Goals:** 2    **Points:** 118

**Transferred to:** Doncaster

In 1970/71 Phil won the 'A' team Player of the Year award and broke into the first team on a permanent basis at the beginning of 1971/72. That season was easily the most momentous of his career. He played in 46 games out of 47, more than anyone else, and had his best try tally with 12. He and Willicombe formed a fine centre partnership, which contributed mightily to Halifax's winning of the John Player Trophy. After scoring in the third-round victory over Barrow, he claimed vital tries in the semi-final against Leeds, a forty-yard interception, which gave Halifax the lead, and in the final at Odsal, when he finished off a move by Bruce Burton and Tony Halmshaw to stretch Halifax's lead from 12-8 to 17-8, effectively killing off Wakefield Trinity's challenge.

In 1972/73 Phil figured in 39 of Halifax's 40 matches and in 34 of 35 in 1974/75. He held a centre spot until the 1976/77 season, when he had a spell on the wing, as Lee Greenwood and Derek Tudball filled the centres. He captained Halifax for part of that season.

By 1977/78 Halifax had dropped to rock bottom and Phil was one of those who had the misfortune to be in the team which lost to Cawoods in the John Player Trophy first round on 23 October 1977. He scored his last try for the club in that ill-starred match, his 218th appearance.

He was transfer-listed at £1,000 in January 1979 and moved to Doncaster, giving them three years' excellent service, making 90 appearances and captaining them in 1979/80. He hardly missed a game at the Dons and developed into a useful loose forward.

Most players are not stars, but the stars often depend on the players surrounding them. Phil Davies could never claim to have been a star but his steady, unspectacular style of centre play helped shore up a Halifax team, which saw far more downs than ups in the decade in which he wore the blue and white.

Halifax paid out £500 to obtain Phil's signature after he played a series of trials for the 'A' team. His first appearance at Thrum Hall saw him substitute the equally new centre David Willicombe on 10 August 1969, when Halifax went down 31-38 to Bradford Northern 'A'. The two young centres would eventually share a fruitful partnership in the first team.

Phil had been a product of Normanton ARL Club and had two brothers: Frank, who won Yorkshire and Wales honours, and Tom, who played professionally with Huddersfield. He was the perfect build for centre – six feet tall and 13st 10lbs – but actually played his first full game for Halifax, after several substitute appearances, on the left wing, scoring a try in a 21-11 win over Hull KR on 30 March 1970.

# Ken Dean & Stan Kielty
Half-backs, 1948-1960, 1946-1958

When rugby league was a game of specialised positions, none was more important than the half-backs – stand-off and scrum-half. Together with the loose forward they were the fulcrum of the side. Halifax have had some wonderful half-back pairings down the years, stretching back to Tommy Grey and Jimmy Hilton in Edwardian days, through to the Welsh wonders Bobby Lloyd and Stuart Prosser, both from Pontypool, a little later, and subsequent coruscating combinations such as Ivor Davies and Gillie Hanson, Wembley winners in 1931, and George Todd and Jack Goodall in the later 1930s.

For many years long-serving half-back partnerships were the backbone of some of the finest teams the game has seen. Pre-war years threw up Shannon and McCue at Widnes, Jenkins and Watkins at Salford and Todd and Thornton at Hunslet. The post-war years produced such gems as Mountford and Bradshaw (Wigan), Price and Helme (Warrington), Horne and Toohey (Barrow), Davies and Ward (Bradford Northern) and a host of others, through to Mullaney and Fox (Featherstone Rovers), Shoebottom and Seabourne (Leeds) and Hardisty and Hepworth (Castleford). All these, and more, were sublime partnerships.

None, however, could have been more mutually dependent than that of Ken Dean and Stan Kielty. The pair became so synonymous with each other that they are known as a solitary entity, the legendary Dean 'n' Kielty – always in that order, despite Stan's seniority. The affection in which the two were, and still are, held has probably never been paralleled in the club's history. It has been reinforced over the near half-century since their retirements by their continuing friendship, close proximity of houses and constant cordial relationships with their fans.

Like most great half-backs of bygone eras, the two were diminutive – 5' 6" and eleven-stoners. Both won county and international honours, although many thought they did not receive their dues at the highest level, for neither won Test status. Temperamentally and in style the two differed, but they complemented each other perfectly.

First on the Thrum Hall scene was Stan, a miner from Castleford. He had played scrum-half for the amateur team Wheldale Colliery before signing for Wakefield Trinity in 1944. The great Herbert Goodfellow barred Stan's way into the first team and he was happy to move to Thrum Hall in October 1946, making his try-scoring debut, along with half-back partner and fellow debutant George Kenny (ex Seghill RU), in a 21-11 victory

*This cartoon appeared in Ken Adams's Sketchbook in the Halifax Courier & Guardian's 'Green Final' edition of 9 May 1953. 'Fax's mercurial half-backs Ken Dean and Stan Kielty are shown as if joined at the hip like Siamese twins. Unfortunately on this occasion Halifax went down 14-24 to St Helens in the 1953 Championship final at Maine Road, Manchester before a crowd of 51,083.*

over York. Stan would go on to make more appearances for the club than anyone. In seven of the twelve full seasons of his time with Halifax he played over 40 games, a remarkable testimony to his durability and doggedness. Of his 481 games, all but one were in the number seven jersey, the exception being when he appeared at left-centre at Salford on 6 December 1947, scoring 'Fax's try in a 5-12 defeat.

In 1947/48 Stan led both Halifax's appearances (38) and try-scoring (13) lists. He came good in the 1948/49 season, again heading the appearances (42 games), scoring one of Halifax's tries in the 8-10 loss to the Kangaroos and being a major figure in 'Fax's drive to the Challenge Cup final. Perhaps his most vital try came in the semi-final at Odsal,

## Ken Dean

**Previous club:** Greetland All Rounders ARL

**Halifax debut:** 6 November 1948 v. Dewsbury

**Final Halifax appearance:** 5 March 1960
   v. Featherstone Rovers

**Appearances:** 394

**Tries:** 89   **Goals:** 65   **Points:** 397

**Transferred to:** Retired

**Honours:** Yorkshire, England

## Stan Kielty

**Previous club:** Wakefield Trinity

**Halifax debut:** 19 October 1946 v. York

**Final Halifax appearance:** 9 September 1958
   v. York  Yorkshire Cup

**Appearances:** 481

**Tries:** 72   **Goals:** 7   **Points:** 230

**Transferred to:** Retired

**Honours:** Yorkshire, England

when Halifax stupefied the game and a 61,875 crowd by beating eventual champions Huddersfield 11-10, Stan's touchdown effectively taking Halifax to Wembley, where they lost to Bradford Northern.

By that time Ken Dean had arrived at Thrum Hall. He was a local lad, who had played league at Battinson Road school, for the Halifax Supporters Under-16s and for St Mary's ARL before being called up for the Army. On demob he had played briefly for Greetland All Rounders but soon signed for Halifax for £300 as a scrum-half. It was there that he played his first three games, deputising for Stan, scoring the first of his 89 tries for the club on his third appearance, at Fartown on Christmas Day 1948. On New Year's Day 1949 Ken moved to stand-off, partnering Stan for the first time in a 6-0 home win against Leeds, 12,000 being in attendance. The pair would go on to play as Halifax's half-backs in 299 games over the following nine years.

Stan was a master craftsman as a scrum-half. He knew all the tricks and a few more besides. He worked in harmony with his loose forward, employing back-flips and set moves, and getting the best out of his pack. Although not the fastest, he was cheeky, mischievous and tough, a real irritant to opponents. He was adept at the grubber kick and was masterful at using the Thrum Hall slope to keep the opposition pinned down. His ability

to steal the ball in the tackle was legendary. Poker-faced Stan was not a man to take your eyes off – he was not a prolific scorer but he was a prolific provider.

Ken was a delightful and exciting player. Quicksilver in attack, he was as quick as anyone over those first vital twenty yards and had twinkling feet and great dodging ability. He was an outstandingly good and clean tackler, admired for his equable nature and sportsmanship. He was also a capable stand-in goal-kicker, and versatile enough to play in all the three-quarters positions, as well as in both half-back berths. In combination he and Stan were almost telepathic and few bettered them.

In 1949/50 the two played their first full season together and were so successful as a link and catalyst that Halifax reached the top four play-offs. Ken scored his first hat-trick in a 20-0 win at Bramley. The following season Stan claimed his only hat-trick, and dropped a goal, in a 46-11 home victory over Hull KR, a game which also saw Ken bag a try and six goals. By then, both were attracting the eyes of the representative selectors. Perhaps surprisingly, the younger Ken was capped first by Yorkshire and England. He won his first Yorkshire cap against Cumberland on 27 September 1950, as partner to Alf Burnell (Hunslet). Stan had to wait a year, making his debut alongside Ken in a 25-3 destruction of the Cumbrians at Craven Park, Hull.

Yorkshire won the County Championship in 1951/52 and would also win it in 1953/54 with the Halifax pair at the heart of the action. Stan would pick up a third winners' medal in 1957/58, partnering Gordon Brown (Leeds) in his last county match, a 25-11 beating of Lancashire at Widnes. Both Stan and Ken played 11 games for Yorkshire, 9 of them together. Ken scored 3 tries for the county but failed to touch down in either of his international appearances. He represented England against Other Nationalities twice, kicking a couple of goals on his debut in a 10-35 loss at Wigan on 11 April 1951. His other appearance was a 12-31 defeat at Fartown on 18 October 1952.

Stan's England debut was delayed until 16 September 1953, when he partnered Willie Horne in a 24-5 pummelling of Wales at St Helens. That was followed on 7 November by a 7-5 win over France at Odsal when Stan scored a seventy-ninth minute match-winning obstruction try, his half-back partner Peter Metcalfe (St Helens) kicking England's two goals. Three weeks later, again in combination with Horne, Stan played his third and final international when Other Nationalities were beaten 30-22 at Wigan in a televised match, as England lifted the European Championship. Ken and Stan were expected to be contenders for the Lions tour in 1954. Indeed Stan was regarded as a certainty and was duly selected as vice-captain to future Thrum Haller Ken Traill, of the White XIII which drew 17-17 with the Red XIII in a tour trial at Headingley on 24 February 1954. When he was overlooked in the final selection, there was mystification. It was probably scant consolation when he was selected as a reserve for the 1954 World Cup behind Gerry Helme and Billy Banks.

On the domestic front Ken and Stan were outstanding figures for Halifax in all their triumphs and near misses of the 1950s. It helped that they played behind one of the best packs in the sport. Even so, their toughness and durability were unquestionable; a combined total of almost 900 matches for the club being proof.

Their first major final together was the Championship final of 1953, when Halifax gave St Helens a tough game at Maine Road before going down 14-24. Halifax won the Yorkshire League in 1952/53 too, Stan appearing in 47 of the season's fixtures and Ken in 43. In 1953/54 Ken topped the appearances with 45, one more than Stan, as Halifax again took the Yorkshire League and endured the agony of losing so narrowly in the Championship and Challenge Cup finals against Warrington. Following those epic encounters they figured together in both games against their conquerors in Belfast and Dublin, where Halifax won 34-15 and 23-11, both scoring tries in the latter match.

1954/55 saw Ken injured for most of the first half the season but he was fit for Halifax's 7-0 victory over Hull in the Yorkshire Cup final at Headingley. Stan missed only one of 'Fax's 44 matches. It said much for the team's power that there was great disappointment that Halifax finished only fourth in the table. They were back on top in 1955/56, however. Ken and Stan orchestrated a victory over the Kiwis and the winning of the Yorkshire Cup and the Yorkshire League. Ken scored one of the most brilliant and crucial tries of his career in the Challenge Cup semi-final at Odsal, where Wigan were beaten 11-10. There was, however, disappointment when they were runners-up again at Wembley against St Helens and versus Hull in the Championship final, their last final together.

In 1956/57 Ken was appointed captain after Ken Traill stepped down. He figured in 43 matches but frequently played in the three-quarters, while Stan made 42 appearances. Their last campaign together was 1957/58, when they picked up their fourth Yorkshire League winners' medals. Stan retired at the close of the season and became 'A' team coach but made a final appearance in a 15-19 home loss to York the following season.

Ken soldiered on through 1959/60, playing against the Australians and in a Yorkshire Cup semi-final against Hull. Ken and Stan later teamed up as coaches at Thrum Hall when Albert Fearnley resigned in 1966.

One final statistic: Between 15 October 1949 and 7 April 1958, there were only five occasions when both Ken and Stan were missing from the Halifax team.

# Terry Dewhirst
Prop, 1965-1979

**Previous club:** Dewsbury Celtic ARL

**Halifax debut:** 25 September 1965 v. Hull

**Final Halifax appearance:** 4 April 1979
    v. Bramley

**Appearances:** 148 + 13 subs

**Tries:** 13   **Goals:** 0   **Points:** 39

**Transferred to:** Bramley (1), retired (2)

As old-fashioned props go, Terry Dewhirst was a typical example – the type that no self-respecting pack could do without in the days when specialism in position and scrimmaging prowess were prime requisites. Terry, or TD, as he was often called, had all the attributes – size and weight (5'11" and 15st 7lbs in his prime), belligerence, the ability to make his hooker look good and a willingness to work hard. In his later days he developed into a forward who could take on defenders and slip out that telling ball, which opened up gaps for support players, and, like most props, to the fans he was a bit of a character.

Terry signed for Halifax from Dewsbury Celtic and he never played anywhere but prop for the club. His signing-on fee was reported to be £200. When Ken Roberts and Charlie Renilson were selected to play for Great Britain against New Zealand at Swinton in the First Test of 1965, Terry was drafted in to the first team and surprised all and sundry with a two-try performance, a feat he would never reproduce for Halifax, apart from in a charity match at Swinton in 1970.

It was not until 1968/69 that he became a first-team regular, playing in over 120 games in the following five seasons, being equally effective at open-side and blind-side prop. His greatest moments with the club came in 1971/72, by which time he was twenty-eight. His front-row combination with Roy Hawksley and Dave Callon proved a potent weapon in Halifax's winning of the John Player Trophy in its inaugural season and the trio contributed mightily to Halifax's drive to the Challenge Cup semi-final, only to experience defeat against Leeds at Odsal.

Less than two years later, however, on 20 January 1974, he played his last game for Halifax for almost five years in a 26-10 win at Blackpool Borough. Terry then became a publican and was eventually signed by Bramley on a free transfer, playing 17 games for them before becoming player-coach at Dewsbury Celtic. He led Celtic to a 13-7 victory over NDLB (Hull Dockers) in the BARLA Yorkshire Cup final in 1977/78, scoring the try which gave his team an 8-7 interval lead. Later that season he was in the Celtic side which gave Vince Karalius's Wigan a very hard time in a first round Challenge Cup-tie, losing only 5-15 before a 4,000 crowd at Mount Pleasant, Batley.

Aged thirty-five, Terry returned to Thrum Hall during Maurice Bamford's reign as coach, reappearing in a 21-9 victory at Leigh Miners Welfare on 23 September 1978 in a first-round Players Trophy match. A pulled muscle curtailed his comeback match to only eleven minutes but he finished his last season with another dozen first-team games to his credit.

# Colin Dixon
Centre, second-row forward, 1961-1968

**Previous club:** Cardiff Junior RU

**Halifax debut:** 30 August 1961 v. Hunslet

**Final Halifax appearance:** 14 December 1968
v. Dewsbury

**Appearances:** 242 + 3 subs

**Tries:** 73   **Goals:** 0   **Points:** 219

**Transferred to:** Salford

**Honours:** Other Nationalities (County),
Wales, Great Britain

There is little doubt that Colin Dixon will eventually be recognised as one of the all-time great players of rugby league. They already know that he was in Halifax and Salford, clubs which benefited immeasurably from his presence in their backs and packs in some of their halcyon days. By the time his twenty-year career ended in 1981 Colin had played a monumental 738 first-class matches, a record bettered by only five men in the history of the sport – Jim Sullivan, Gus Risman, Neil Fox, Jeff Grayshon and Graham Idle. The way the game is presently structured will almost certainly ensure that no other player will reach the 700-appearances mark.

The manner in which Colin played makes his longevity even more remarkable. He was a whirlwind, always at the centre of the action, playing the game as hard and fast as he could, which was exceedingly hard and pretty fast. His career as a representative player lasted a phenomenal eighteen years, which is another indication of an outstanding talent. Moreover, he was versatile enough to have played at international levels at centre, second-row and loose forward, while he also propped for Salford in one of his four Lancashire Cup final appearances.

Halifax fans remember Colin as a rampaging centre partner to Johnny Freeman or the perfect second-row foil to Terry Fogerty. Wherever he played Colin delivered the goods – all-out effort, fierce defence, an ability to shatter the defensive line and the strength and pace to score from long or short distances and he was spectacular, to put it mildly. His power-speed ratio could rarely have been emulated. He was a hard man to put down and as he matured he became adept at releasing the ball from the tackle.

A native of Cardiff, Colin played rugby union at South Church Street School, where the great Gus Risman had also been a pupil, and for Cardiff Schools and Cardiff Youth. Among his contemporaries were David Watkins and Jim Mills, with whom he would later play professionally. Colin came to Halifax as a scrum-half aged seventeen but he was already too big to be considered for that position as a league player. Halifax decided that he would be an ideal successor to Geoff Palmer as Freeman's centre.

His initial game with the first team was in the Charity Cup match at Fartown on 12 August 1961. Huddersfield were beaten 18-13 and Colin helped Freeman to a hat-trick. In only his fourth senior game he played for a combined Halifax-Huddersfield XIII which lost 11-31 to the New Zealanders. By the close of his first season he had played 19 games and scored 3 tries. It was clear he was going places but injuries and an influx of new faces restricted him to just 15 games (5 tries) in the following season. Despite his tender years Colin was selected to play for a Welsh XIII against France at Toulouse.

The 1963/64 campaign saw him break into the first team permanently. In 36 games he scored 14 tries and in the early part of the season he won his first medal when 'Fax beat Featherstone Rovers in the Yorkshire Cup final. In the latter part of the season he was tried in the forwards with devastating effect. His pulverising running in a sublime back row with Fogerty and Renilson helped Halifax to lift the Eastern Division title, Colin being a try-scorer in the final against Castleford.

The 1964/65 season saw Colin playing mostly in the second row and his form was so impressive he won the Player of the Year award. Halifax won the Championship with Colin being a major strike force in an irresistible pack. The next season took Halifax back to the Championship final, only to be heavily defeated by St Helens. By then Colin had reverted to centre and he figured there for most of the following two years.

Halifax were in decline but Colin was improving. In 1966/67 he was ever-present in 39 fixtures, was again elected Player of the Year and scored 16 tries, his best tally for the club. He was appointed captain in February 1967 and retained the position until he left Thrum Hall twenty-two months later. Of the 82 games Halifax played in the period of his captaincy, Colin missed just seven and no one was in any doubt as to where he led from – the front. He was here, there and everywhere, despite supposedly being in the centres for most of that period. In 1967/68 he figured in 40 of Halifax's 43 fixtures, led the team

*Colin Dixon scores one of his 73 tries for Halifax. This one is against Castleford in 1967. His wing partner Johnny Freeman is in the background.*

against the Australians and took them into the Top Sixteen play-offs. His 15 tries was bettered only by David Jones (16).

Colin's form in 1968/69 was magnificent. He had returned to the pack and was so outstanding that he won Wales and Great Britain caps. By December he had taken Halifax into the top four, had scored 10 tries in 19 games, including his first hat-trick. He was inspirational and unstoppable. At that point Halifax did the unthinkable and sold him to Salford for a world record fee of £15,000, which included the acquisition of winger Mike Kelly. By the season's end Halifax had slumped to eighteenth in the table. Colin went on to play at Wembley in 1969, won two Championships and played in six other major finals with Salford. He toured with the Lions in 1974 and with Wales in 1975, was a member of the Great Britain World Cup winning squad in 1972 and earned 14 Test caps and 15 Wales caps. His career ended with Hull KR, for whom he played his last game at Thrum Hall on 20 April 1981.

# Paul Dixon

Second-row forward, loose forward, 1985-1988

**Previous club:** Huddersfield

**Halifax debut:** I September 1985 v. Oldham

**Final Halifax appearance:** 26 December 1988 v. Leeds

**Appearances:** 127 + 2 subs

**Tries:** 52   **Goals:** 0   **Points:** 208

**Transferred to:** Leeds

**Honours:** Yorkshire, Great Britain

There is no doubt that Paul Dixon ranks among the very best forwards to have represented Halifax, and that is saying a great deal. Paul signed for Halifax from his local team Huddersfield, although he had only recently finished playing on loan with Oldham. He had played his amateur rugby with Underbank, had gained BARLA test honours against France at Under-19 level and was almost twenty-three when Halifax signed him, on 16 August 1985.

At Thrum Hall Paul developed into one of the most exciting and entertaining forwards of the era. He had everything. He was not the biggest forward – 5' 11" and about 14st 12lb – but he had enormous strength and the ability to puncture defences almost at will. He was an expert at spinning off tackles and bursting through the defensive line, which often resulted in runaway tries, sometimes from his own half. While he was quite capable of extraordinary attacking skills, he had bags of stamina and was a workhorse in defence.

Paul scored Halifax's only try on his debut, a 12-12 draw with Oldham, and went onto rattle up 52 tries in only 129 appearances, an outstanding ratio for a second-rower. His career tally topped 150 tries. In his first two seasons at Halifax Paul figured at loose forward more than at second row, although he

seemed more at home in the latter position.

In 1985/86 he and Gary Stephens played more games (37) than anyone and he finished as the leading try-scorer with 13, including one against Featherstone Rovers in the last match of the season, when Halifax clinched the Championship. He appeared in Halifax's Premiership final defeat by Warrington but had better luck a few months later when Halifax beat Castleford in the Charity Shield.

Season 1986/87 brought him top position in the appearances list with 41, in which he claimed 14 tries. In Halifax's run to Challenge Cup final triumph over St Helens, Paul was a try-scorer in the second and third round victories over Hunslet and Hull KR. His performances throughout the season brought him the Player of the Year award.

In 1987/88 he retained the award, a distinction only previously achieved by Terry Langton. He scored a try in Halifax's defeat by Wigan in the Charity Shield and went on to equal Derrick Schofield's club forward try-scoring record of 17 in a season. In one spell he bagged 13 tries in 13 games, including five tries in the first three rounds of the Challenge Cup, Halifax going on to Wembley, where Wigan defeated them. The 1988 Challenge Cup was Paul's last major final for Halifax. He played on at Thrum Hall in 1988/89, scoring a sensational long-distance try against the touring French international side. His transfer to Leeds came as a huge disappointment to the fans, his exchange for Paul Medley and John Lyons being rated at £140,000.

# Graham Eadie
Full-back, 1986-1988

**Previous club:** Manly

**Halifax debut:** 31 August 1986
   *v.* Featherstone Rovers

**Final Halifax appearance:** 25 September
   1988 *v.* Hull KR

**Appearances:** 74

**Tries:** 29   **Goals:** 24   **Points:** 164

**Transferred to:** Retired

**Honours:** New South Wales, Australia

When Graham 'Wombat' Eadie retired from Australian rugby league after Manly's defeat by Parramatta in the 1983 Grand Final, he was firmly enshrined in rugby league folklore as one of Australia's greatest full-backs. He had played in 12 Tests, had toured as a Kangaroo in 1973 and 1978 and had been a World Cup winner in 1975 and 1977. He had won four Grand Finals and lost two with Manly, for whom he had scored a record 1,917 points (71 tries, 847 goals, 3 drop goals) in 237 appearances. When he retired no one had scored more first-grade points than Graham and his 2,070 points in all grades for Manly remains a record today.

His signing for Halifax three years later came as something of a shock. Obviously, he was older, slower and heavier – getting on for 15st – so it was a gamble for both club and player. That it paid off was unquestionable. Graham became as big a hero in Halifax as he was in Australia and brought happy memories to all those fortunate enough to have seen his all too brief career at Thrum Hall.

Graham succeeded Queenslander 'Smokin' Joe' Kilroy as Halifax full-back. Kilroy had been a charismatic figure in Halifax's winning of the Championship in 1985/86, so explosive and entertaining that he was thought by many to be irreplaceable. No problem. Graham made up for his lack of mobility with anticipation, nous and skill. His positional play was flawless and followers who witnessed his Halifax career swear he only dropped one

ball in his time at the club. His timing was so fine that he rattled up 20 tries in 1986/87 in 36 appearances, eclipsing Tony Hepworth's club record for a full-back in a season.

His contribution to Halifax's taking of the Challenge Cup was tremendous. He scored a try in the first round at Fulham, two against Hunslet in the second round and another against Hull KR in the third. In the final at Wembley against St Helens, Graham had one of the games of his life, making several try-saving tackles, scoring a fifty-first-minute try and winning the Lance Todd Trophy.

In 1987/88 Graham captained the side taking them back to Wembley but this time with no fairy tale ending as Wigan overwhelmed Halifax 32-12. His season's contribution had been 9 tries, including a hat-trick at Leigh, and 13 goals in 33 appearances.

His stay at Halifax ended in near farce, however. Having appointed him player-coach for 1988/89, Halifax perversely brought in Ross Strudwick as coach, from which point everything at Thrum Hall went downhill. Graham resigned having played his last three games for the club at stand-off. He left Halifax as an authentic idol of the crowd. The new coach presided over Halifax's relegation.

**Previous club:** Oldham

**Halifax debut:** 18 November 1950
  *v.* Featherstone Rovers

**Final Halifax appearance:** 1 September 1956
  *v.* Dewsbury  Yorkshire Cup

**Appearances:** 207

**Tries:** 39   **Goals:** 0   **Points:** 117

**Transferred to:** Featherstone Rovers

**Honours:** Yorkshire

There is no doubt that Albert Fearnley was one of the most significant figures in the history of Halifax Rugby League Club – firstly, as a fiery forward during the 1950s and, secondly, as the coach to the great team of the 1960s. He used to claim that he had won more medals as a Thrum Haller than any other man. He was not boasting but simply expressing his pride in the achievement and his affection for the club.

Albert was a Bradfordian, who began his career with Bradford Northern Juniors and started his professional career with Rochdale Hornets in 1946. He remained a Hornet until 1949, playing 95 games and scoring 20 tries. He played mostly at loose forward but had one game as winger. In 1948 he played in Hornets' Challenge Cup semi-final defeat by Wigan. It would be six more years before he reached Wembley. He was transferred to Oldham in November 1949 for the considerable sum of £1,500 plus forward Tom Rostron. His stay at Watersheddings lasted a year (28 appearances, 5 tries) before Halifax signed him for £1,650 in November 1950.

Oldham had utilised Albert as a second-rower but he began his career with Halifax at loose forward, making his debut along with local hooker Raymond Illingworth in an 18-6

win at Featherstone. Halifax soon realised that he was better suited to the second row. The presence of Frank Birkin and the arrival of Des Clarkson meant that loose forward was well covered and in 1951/52 Albert settled into a tremendous second-row partnership with Les White. That season Albert was the club's top try-scoring forward with 8 in 34 games. He also made his first appearance against a touring team when Halifax beat the New Zealanders 18-12.

In 1952/53 Albert was at the top of his form, again leading the forward try-scorers with a dozen in 43 outings. He scored tries in four consecutive matches, and he must have derived special pleasure from scoring twice in 'Fax's exciting 18-16 home victory over Bradford Northern in the Championship semi-final. Halifax fell 14-24 to St Helens in the final at Maine Road but Albert collected his first winners' medal as Halifax lifted the Yorkshire League Championship.

The 1953/54 season brought Albert a new second-row partner in the dashing Derrick Schofield. It also brought Halifax another Yorkshire League Championship and the opportunity to achieve a League and Cup double, only to lose agonisingly to Warrington in both major finals. In the Challenge Cup Albert was a try-scorer in the first round against Dewsbury and in the semi-final against Hunslet at Odsal. His first appearance at Wembley ended in a 4-4 draw and 'Fax lost the replay at Odsal and then

*Albert Fearnley stops his man at Fartown in 1953. Jack Wilkinson peers over the breaking scrum, while rival scrum-halves Stan Kielty and Billy Banks await developments.*

were beaten by one point at Maine Road in the Championship final. Albert played in the two exhibition games against Warrington, in Belfast, where he scored a try, and Dublin. Both games were won.

In 1954/55 Albert reverted to loose forward when Des Clarkson was transferred. He was less suited to that position but gave everything. His forte was the second row, where his enthusiasm, penchant for try-scoring, boundless energy, hard tackling and strong running were inspirational. Albert, 5' 11" and 14st 4lbs, was an extremely competitive player, sometimes too competitive according to his critics and his robustness occasionally got him into trouble. He was suspended for the 1954 Yorkshire Cup final but got his winners' medal, having appeared in the first two rounds.

Albert made up for missing the 1954 Yorkshire Cup final in 1955, when he was loose forward in the 10-10 drawn final against Hull at Headingley and in the replay at Odsal which Halifax won 7-0. He also picked up his third Yorkshire League Championship winners' medal in 1955/56. In the Challenge Cup he again played at Wembley, in the second row with Les Pearce, when Halifax lost 2-13 to St Helens. His disappointment must have been immense when he was left out of the team which lost to Hull in the

Championship final a week later.

Albert only played once again for Halifax after that Wembley defeat. Along with Tommy Lynch, who retired through injury, Albert was the first of the great 1950s team to leave the club. He was transferred to Featherstone Rovers for £750 and, ironically, made his debut for them when they beat Halifax 22-9 at Post Office Road on 8 September 1956. He was quickly made skipper of Rovers, for whom he made 67 appearances, scoring 18 tries and 2 goals. In two years with Rovers he revitalised them, taking them to the Challenge Cup semi-final in 1958. His last season as a player, 1958/59, saw him player-coach to Batley, where he appeared mainly at blind-side prop and led them to a Yorkshire Cup semi-final appearance.

His later coaching career was extremely successful. His major triumphs were with Halifax in the 1960s. Albert also took charge of Bradford Northern, Keighley and Blackpool Borough, taking the latter to an unlikely promotion to Division One in 1978/79. Albert was an evangelist for the sport, making major contributions to the grassroots game, schools and development through the National Coaching Scheme. As early as May 1959 he was coaching Italians in Treviso and later coached in the U.S.

# John Fieldhouse
Prop, second-row forward, 1991-1995

**Previous club:** Oldham

**Halifax debut:** 15 September 1991
    *v.* Wakefield Trinity  Yorkshire Cup

**Final Halifax appearance:** 10 December 1995
    *v.* St Helens  Regal Trophy

**Appearances:** 102 + 9 subs

**Tries:** 13  **Goals:** 0  **Points:** 52

**Transferred to:** South Wales

**Honours:** Lancashire, Great Britain Under-
    24s, Great Britain

There were few dull moments when John Fieldhouse was on the field. His professional career, which stretched from 1979 to 1997, took in Warrington, Widnes, St Helens, Oldham, South Wales and Whitehaven, plus a brief sojourn at Orrell RU. His five-season stint with Halifax came after he had already put in twelve years as a pro. The enthusiasm and effort he exuded, however, were those of a much younger player.

Solidly built at over fifteen stones and six feet tall, the former Wigan St Patricks product was the type of forward fans could not help noticing. He played vigorously, tackling with power although not with textbook style but he certainly kept coming at opposing packs. He was not a great distributor but probably thought he was, as he was always willing to take risks. Sometimes they paid off, sometimes not, but John definitely made life interesting. He always led from the front.

Before coming to Thrum Hall John had been a Lancashire Cup-winner with Warrington in 1982 and had been in the St Helens team which lost at Wembley in 1987 to Halifax. A year later he was in Saints' Premiership final runners-up side against Widnes, while in 1990 he had been a winner

in Oldham's Second Division Premiership final success over Hull KR. In 1985 and 1986 John won 7 caps for Great Britain and was Man of the Series against the 1985 Kiwis.

Consequently, when Halifax paid £25,000 in 1991 to Oldham for his services they were acquiring a lot of experience and nous. His debut saw him score a try in the last ever Yorkshire Cup-tie to be staged at Thrum Hall, when he partnered Richard Milner in the second row. Most of his early games with Halifax were played as a second-rower but from 1992 he operated mainly as blind-side prop, forming a fearsome duo with skipper Karl Harrison at open-side.

Halifax did not win anything tangible in John's time with them but they were competitive and often played entertaining rugby, with John Fieldhouse providing more than his share of the entertainment. John's value to the side was well illustrated in 1992/93 when he was made captain in nine matches when Karl Harrison temporarily relinquished the role.

In 1994, aged thirty-two, John was in the last Halifax team to face the Australians and played well in a 12-26 defeat. Later that season he was controversially sent off in Halifax's 14-18 loss against his old team St Helens at Knowsley Road. His last game for Halifax was also away against Saints in a Regal Trophy tie where his jaw was broken – a sad end for a popular Thrum Haller.

# Terry Fogerty
Second-row forward, open-side prop, 1961-1973

**Previous club:** Saddleworth Rangers ARL

**Halifax debut:** 25 March 1961 v. Batley

**Final Halifax appearance:** 8 September 1973 v. Huyton

**Appearances:** 296 + 2 subs

**Tries:** 65   **Goals:** 1   **Points:** 197

**Transferred to:** Wigan (1), Rochdale Hornets (2)

**Honours:** Commonwealth XIII, Lancashire, Great Britain

Terrence Heywood Fogerty was born in Glossop on 29 June 1944. He had rugby league in his blood, his father, Les, having played on the wing five times for Swinton in April 1946. Terry joined Saddleworth Rangers and made such an impression at loose forward that Halifax signed him just after his sixteenth birthday, despite competition from Oldham. His talent was such that within nine months he was given his first-team debut. The only younger players to have appeared for the club were Tom Schofield (1917) and Alan Prescott (1943), both in wartime rugby.

A fair-haired giant at over six feet tall and eventually over sixteen stones, Terry had far more than mere bulk, useful though that was. As a creative, attacking forward it is hard to think of any better who has played in the blue and white hoops. Terry was so effective with the ball in his hands that no-one cared too much about his tackling deficiencies. Sometimes he would be almost anonymous, he would have the odd stinker of a game, and he had an infuriating habit of losing possession, probably because he was thinking three moves ahead. All these traits were forgiven, however, because Terry was a genius. He won games and captivated crowds. When on top form, he was spellbinding.

Terry could conjure up openings where none appeared to exist, he could deliver killer passes when other players would not have even contemplated passing, and he had a

body-wobble which had players falling helplessly before they got near him. He was extremely quick too, making him a prolific try-scorer as well as a consummate try-maker.

Before he was nineteen Terry had played 32 first-team games and been a professional for three years. He was settled at second-row. The 1963/64 season saw him earn a permanent place in the team, playing in 36 matches. That campaign brought him winners' medals for the Yorkshire Cup and for the Eastern Division Championship. He was mostly alongside Ken Roberts but towards the end of the season Terry was paired with Colin Dixon, the two perfectly complementing each other. Together with loose forward Charlie Renilson they made a devastating trio. They first played together as a unit in Lewis Jones' final game for Leeds at Headingley on 30 March 1964. A few weeks later they were dominant when 'Fax beat Castleford 20-12 at Fartown to lift the Eastern Division title.

In 1964/65 Terry made 40 appearances, scoring 9 tries, including two in a breathtaking performance at Castleford in the Championship semi-final, Halifax winning 26-18. The next week at Swinton, Halifax won the Championship, beating St Helens. Terry played superbly, becoming the first

*The Keighley defence wonders what Terry Fogerty will do next in a game at Thrum Hall in 1966. Also pictured are Dave Harrison, Paul Daley, John Burnett and Barry Robinson.*

player to win the Harry Sunderland Trophy.

The following season saw Terry chosen as Halifax's Player of the Year and his representative career take off. He won selection for a Commonwealth XIII against New Zealand at Crystal Palace, Lancashire caps against Cumberland and the Kiwis and selection for the 1966 Australasian tour. Before touring he played in an unsuccessful Championship final against St Helens, scoring one try and having one disallowed. On tour he played in 20 of the 30 fixtures and scored 5 tries. He was substitute for the first Ashes test at Sydney and for both tests in New Zealand, making his debut in Britain's 22-14 victory in the second test at Auckland.

Halifax succumbed to Wigan's offer of £7,500 for Terry in December 1966, when he had made 160 appearances for the club (29 tries), despite still being only twenty-two. He remained with Wigan for almost three years, playing Test rugby against France in 1967 and figuring in Wigan's 1968 Floodlit Trophy final triumph over St Helens.

Much to the 'Fax fans' delight, Halifax re-signed Terry for £5,500 and he made his second debut in a 28-15 win at Bramley on 20 September 1969, scoring a try. Halifax were rebuilding after the triumphs of the mid-1960s

and Terry was regarded as the foundation stone for the hoped-for revival. He had lost none of his creativity but he was not blessed with such splendid colleagues as in his first spell. Even so, great days did come again in 1971/72, when Terry played a big part in Halifax's achievement in winning the inaugural John Player Trophy and reaching the semi-finals of the Challenge Cup.

In 1972/73 Terry played some of his best rugby despite Halifax being in mid-table. He played in 39 of the team's 40 fixtures and was Player of the Year. His tally of 16 tries has rarely been bettered by a Halifax forward and 12 were scored from prop, a club record. He scored his only hat-trick in 'Fax's record 76-8 victory at Hunslet in a first-round Yorkshire Cup-tie. Towards the end of the season he became captain when Tony Halmshaw joined Rochdale, only to follow him to Hornets at the start of the following season, Halifax receiving £7,000 for him. With Rochdale Terry appeared in a second John Player Trophy final, losing to Warrington, and won another test cap against France in 1974.

Terry's sons Adam and Jason also played professionally. Adam followed his father to Halifax, and later St Helens, while Jason joined Huddersfield.

# Frank Fox
Open-side prop, 1959-1963

**Previous club:** Shaw Cross ARL

**Halifax debut:** 15 August 1959
  *v.* Featherstone Rovers

**Final Halifax appearance:** 2 November 1963
  *v.* Featherstone Rovers  Yorkshire Cup
  final

**Appearances:** 130

**Tries:** 6  **Goals:** 0  **Points:** 18

**Transferred to:** Hull Kingston Rovers

**Honours:** Yorkshire

A product of Wakefield Schools and Shaw Cross amateur rugby league, Frank Fox joined Halifax for £500 in May 1959. He was only nineteen but he was pitched into the first team at open-side prop, extraordinarily young for that position. It helped that he was already six feet tall and 14st 7lbs and would get considerably bigger, but he had the task of stepping into the boots of legendary props John Thorley and Jack Wilkinson.

Frank was not an eye-catcher. He just got on with the hard work of scrummaging, tackling and taking up the ball. He did those jobs so well that he more or less bypassed the usual apprenticeship of playing in the reserves. He did not often score but claimed his first try in a splendid 8-4 victory at Swinton on 20 February 1960. In that game Halifax fielded what was believed to be one of the youngest front rows ever to have played the game – Frank (20), Trevor Taylor (22) and Roger Crabtree (19).

In his second season, 1960/61, Frank appeared in 38 matches, including Halifax's encounter with the 1960 New Zealand World Cup team, which the tourists won 18-12. He was a member of the pack which took Halifax to the Challenge Cup semi-finals in 1961, scoring a crucial try in 'Fax's 8-0 first round win at Hunslet. Workington Town (4-0) and Rochdale Hornets (18-5) were then beaten before 'Fax lost 10-19 to Wigan at Swinton.

On 9 September Frank scored his only try of the 1961/62 season but it allowed Halifax to beat Oldham (7-5) for the first time for a decade. Pickings were lean for Halifax in this period but they did qualify for the newly formed First Division in 1962/63, when Frank made 35 appearances, as Halifax also made the semi-finals of the Yorkshire Cup and Eastern Division Championship.

In 1963/64 Halifax at last became a trophy-winning team again and it was somewhat ironic that Frank should play his last game for the club in the 1963 Yorkshire Cup final victory over Featherstone Rovers at Wakefield. He was on top form in the early months of that season, winning selection, alongside hooker John Shaw, for Yorkshire, who beat the Australians 11-5 at Craven Park, Hull on 18 September. He retained his place in the team which met Cumberland at Wakefield the following week. It was a big surprise, therefore, when he was transferred to Hull KR for £3,500, when seemingly approaching the height of his powers.

Frank had four years at Rovers, helping them to the Yorkshire Cup in 1966, and making 101 appearances. Another three years and 65 appearances followed at Castleford, who reached the finals of the Challenge Cup (winners) and Championship (runners-up) in 1969. Frank was a substitute for both games.

**Previous club:** Manly

**Halifax debut:** 25 February 1967 v. Hunslet

**Final Halifax appearance:** 9 March 1971
v. Barrow

**Appearances:** 108 + 2 subs

**Tries:** 6   **Goals:** 0   **Points:** 18

**Transferred to:** Returned to Australia

In the days before the Australian invasions of the 1980s, Halifax had very little experience of fielding Australians. The only notable Aussies to have graced Thrum Hall had been wingers Fred Tottey (22 games) just before the Second World War and Lionel Williamson (10 games) in 1964/65. Ian Foye lasted much longer, putting in four years.

A Sydney policeman, Ian had played under coach Harry Bath at Balmain in 1962 and 1964 and then moved to Manly in 1965. When he decided to try his luck in England he had originally gone to Barrow but ended up at Thrum Hall instead. Halifax had to pay Manly £400 before he could be signed on 17 February 1967. He played for the reserves the same evening at Castleford. When Ian arrived at Halifax they had not won for ten games and had just lost to Bramley at home for the first time in seventy-one years. With Ian's introduction they won seven and drew one of their next eight games.

Ian Foye was tall for a hooker at almost six feet and he weighed 14st but he couldn't half hook! In those days there could still be up to forty contested scrums per game and a proficient hooker was a vital commodity. In his first game he won the scrums 15-9 as Halifax beat Hunslet 23-19 and thereafter the *Halifax Courier* would recite a triumphant litany of his conquests over the best hookers the game had to offer. Halifax won surprisingly at Featherstone, Ian winning the scrums 23-13, before out-hooking Test player Johnny Ward 16-10 at Castleford and so it went on… 'Foye won the scrums'.

In pure ball-winning terms Halifax have had some great hookers – Harry Field, Alvin Ackerley and John Shaw, for example – but whether they were better than Ian is a moot point. Defensively too Ian was a Trojan. He was fortunate enough to have some good props in his early days at Thrum Hall such as Jim Mills, Jack Scroby and Stuart Kelley, the latter having relinquished the hooking spot.

Halifax never finished higher than tenth in Ian's time and the nearest he got to winning a medal was an appearance in the Yorkshire Cup semi-final against Leeds in 1968. He was unfortunate to miss Halifax's game against the Kangaroos in 1967 but played for Halifax against the British World Cup team in 1968, when Tom van Vollenhoven guested for Britain in his last game.

Like most hookers worth their salt, Ian was sent off a few times, usually for technical offences and often in tandem with the opposing hooker. In 1968/69 he was ordered off three times, including in the Charity Cup match against Huddersfield, along with Test hooker Don Close. It came, as they say, with the territory.

# Johnny Freeman
Left-winger, 1954-1967

**Previous club:** Cardiff International Athletic Club RU

**Halifax debut:** 4 December 1954 v. Wigan

**Final Halifax appearance:** 27 March 1967 v. Oldham

**Appearances:** 396

**Tries:** 290   **Goals:** 15   **Points:** 900

**Transferred to:** Retired

**Honours:** Welsh XIII

Halifax signed Johnny Freeman from Cardiff junior rugby union in 1954 as a centre three-quarter but he went on to become the club's most prolific try-scorer as a left wingman. Johnny became Halifax's greatest try-scorer on 5 October 1963 when he scored a hat-trick against York at Thrum Hall in a 23-9 victory in the old Eastern Division Championship. Those three tries took him past Arthur Daniels' club record of 215 and Johnny went on to amass 290. No one has come remotely close to his figures subsequently.

Johnny had all the attributes required for a top-class winger. He was six feet tall, weighed 12st 7lbs and he was practically uncatchable if given any space. He could have been a fine sprinter. He did not just run straight, however, for he had a good side-step and a tremendous swerve, plus the facility for breaking out of tackles. His acceleration was deceptive for opponents who thought they had him covered and he used the jackhammer hand-off well. He also had neat lines in interceptions and kick-and-chase tries. Johnny scored most of his tries for Halifax in the pavilion corner at Thrum Hall, zipping along the touchline, often from inside his own '25'. Fans called them 'Freeman specials' and they came to expect near-miracles from him.

After a stuttering start to his professional career Johnny proved so sensational as a try-scorer that by 1958 he was rated as the world's best winger by the *Rugby League Gazette*. His first season came to an abrupt end after just four games when he dislocated his shoulder at Warrington on 5 February 1955. He fought his way back into Halifax's star-studded team the following season, however, eventually replacing Dai Bevan on the left flank. In 22 games he touched down 21 times and began a partnership with centre Geoff Palmer which flourished for the next five years. In 1955/56 he picked up a Yorkshire League Championship winners' medal and played at Wembley, becoming a passenger for much of the game when he collided with a photographer, 'Fax losing 2-13 to St Helens. The following week he scored in the Championship final loss to Hull.

In 1956/57 Johnny really got going. He broke Billy Williams's club record by rattling up 48 tries in 45 matches, in a campaign when Halifax dropped from second to twelfth. Among his best performances was a hat-trick against Billy Boston, when Halifax lost 9-25 at Wigan, while he also scored four tries twice. He was even more deadly as 1957/58 unfolded. He scored five tries against Dewsbury and five further hat-tricks. By 21 December 1957 he had cut a swathe through practically all opposition in piling up 38 tries in 20 matches and was on course to match

*There was no stopping Johnny Freeman on this occasion. Dewsbury's defence is about to be outrun as Johnny flashes down the main-stand touchline.*

Albert Rosenfeld's all-time record of 80 tries in a season. Then he injured his knee in scoring his second try at Batley, not playing again for nearly a year. The injury certainly cost him a tour with the Lions in 1958. When he was injured Johnny had gathered 109 tries for Halifax in 91 games. The rugby league world was at his feet. It was scant consolation that he won another Yorkshire League winner's medal for the 1957/58 season.

Although he was never quite as devastating after his return, Johnny still provided excitement and tries. In 1959/60 he claimed 25 tries in 34 games and the following season 29 in 40. Included was one against Wigan at Swinton in the 1961 semi-final of the Challenge Cup, the nearest he would come to returning to Wembley. At the close of the 1960/61 season Geoff Palmer retired but he was fortunate to get a new partner in the shape of Colin Dixon. The two formed a powerful and menacing combination for most of the rest of Johnny's career.

Johnny continued to top the Halifax try-scorers. He had 19 in 1961/62, 23 in 1962/63, 22 in 1963/64 and 28 in 1964/65. Halifax were becoming a force again and Johnny was the bridge between the great days of the mid-1950s and the side of the mid-1960s. In 1963/64 he was a star turn in Halifax's seizure of the Yorkshire Cup and the Eastern Division Championship. The 1964/65 season was even better with Johnny finishing second to Wigan's Trevor Lake in the try-scoring lists and picking up a Championship winners' medal when Halifax defeated St Helens at Swinton. Halifax also took the Mackeson Trophy as the top points scorers.

Johnny's last great season was 1965/66. He topped the appearances lists with 42 and the try-scorers with 18, and appeared in Halifax's bruising repeat Championship final against St Helens at Swinton. A runners-up medal as Halifax lost 12-35 was his last. Johnny carried on for another season and enjoyed a club-record testimonial of £1,013 19s.

It is doubtful if any winger has provided the Halifax faithful with more thrills. He would walk into any test team today but his injury in 1957 and Mick Sullivan being Britain's left-winger for a decade conspired to keep him from the highest representative honours. He appeared once for a Welsh XIII against France in 1963, but no caps were awarded.

# Graham Garrod

Centre, 1978-1985

**Previous club:** Bradford Northern

**Halifax debut:** 20 August 1978 v. Batley Yorkshire Cup

**Final Halifax appearance:** 10 November 1985 v. Leeds

**Appearances:** 212 + 11 subs

**Tries:** 67   **Goals:** 0   **Points:** 220

**Transferred to:** Retired

Graham Garrod joined Halifax on 7 July 1978 together with his Bradford Northern teammate, Derek Howard, a bustling winger, who was very popular at Thrum Hall before injury brought an early end to his career. The double deal cost Halifax £3,500 and Graham certainly gave value for money, whatever percentage of the fee he constituted. Graham was part of the extensive Bradford connection created by coach Maurice Bamford, as he resurrected Halifax from the dead.

Graham had come up through the Colts at Odsal but in four years had only played for the first team 24 times. Once he arrived at Halifax he was hardly ever out of the side. Graham proved to be a revelation. He was totally reliable, both in attack and defence. Well-built at six feet tall and 13st 7lb, Graham was a tower of strength in the middle backs. Against all the conventions, his tackling focused on opponents' upper bodies – a risky business – but he was rarely shaken off as his victims were wrapped up ball and all. Super League tackling would have been right up his street. On attack he scored many notable tries, many long-distance efforts, and he had plenty of speed.

In 1978/79 Halifax went close to promotion with Graham playing in all 33 of their fixtures, which included a near miss in the Yorkshire Cup, when York scraped home 4-2 in the semi-final at Thrum Hall. The following season Graham was again ever-present with 36 appearances, all at right-centre, a very rare achievement. Halifax went one better by reaching the final of the

Yorkshire Cup, losing 6-15 to Leeds at Headingley, and winning promotion to Division One. They also fought their way to the semi-final of the Challenge Cup via Featherstone Rovers, Barrow and Wakefield Trinity before losing to Hull KR. Graham was the leading try-scorer with 17, including hat-tricks in successive league matches at Whitehaven and at home to Swinton.

For five seasons promotion and relegation alternated but Graham was a constant. In 1981/82, a promotion season, Graham was moved to stand-off and excelled in partnership with Terry Langton, finishing as top try-scorer again with 18, at one stage scoring in five consecutive games.

In 1983/84, another promotion season, he figured largely back at centre but was drafted to second row, alongside Brett Greenwood, in a vital 12-10 victory at Carlisle on 26 February 1984. It was his only appearance in the pack in his career.

When the Australian invasion occurred in 1984/85 Graham was one of the few English players who maintained a place in the Halifax side. He played on into the following season and, although he made his last appearance for the club in an 18-18 home draw against Leeds on 10 November 1985, his 10 appearances in league fixtures was sufficient to merit a well-deserved Championship-winners' medal, a just reward for an excellent clubman.

# Wilf George
Left-winger, 1986-1991

**Previous club:** Widnes

**Halifax debut:** 16 February 1986 v. Oldham

**Final Halifax appearance:** 13 October 1991 v. Salford

**Appearances:** 138 + 3 subs

**Tries:** 75  **Goals:** 0  **Points:** 300

**Transferred to:** Batley

Some players achieve a type of cult status at certain clubs which they do not at others. It is often difficult to define what makes some players special in the eyes of supporters but occasionally there is a rapport between fans and players which is infectious. Halifax have had a number of folk heroes. George Standidge and John Bentley immediately spring to mind but it is doubtful if anyone was ever more popular at Thrum Hall than Wilf George. The crowd simply loved Wilf.

There was always a bit of fun and entertainment in the offing when Wilf was in action. He was quite capable of making errors but he was equally capable of doing something extraordinary, which endeared him to the fans. Wilf was not the greatest winger to have played for the blue and whites but he was a very good one. He certainly had size at 6' 1" and 14st 10lbs and he had the power and pace to carry him long distances. He was an extremely difficult man to stop when he had set his sights on the corner. Anyone who saw him score a fabulous try in a Challenge Cup-tie for Huddersfield at Thrum Hall in 1982

would have been tempted to compare him with Johnny Freeman – praise indeed.

Wilf arrived at Thrum Hall in February 1986, a £13,000 buy from Widnes. He played in the final gripping ten matches of the season, scoring one of the tries in the 13-13 draw with Featherstone Rovers which gave Halifax the Championship. Unfortunately, injury prevented him from playing in the Premiership final against Warrington.

Season 1986/87 was particularly good for Wilf, who began by scoring a try in the Charity Shield victory over Castleford and scored his first hat-trick for Halifax in a 38-23 Players Trophy victory over York. He played in all of Halifax's Challenge Cup-ties, scoring in the first round at Fulham and going over for a thrilling touchdown at Wembley in the defeat of St Helens.

In 1987/88 he again played in the Charity Shield and twice scored four tries in a match, against Hunslet and against Heworth in the first round of the Challenge Cup. Halifax again got to Wembley but Wilf was injured. He missed most of the 1988/89 season too, Halifax suffering relegation.

In 1989/90 he claimed 24 tries in 30 games, his best return, including another four-try haul against Whitehaven. Halifax reached the final of the Regal Trophy, Wilf contributing mightily with six tries in the opening three rounds. The following season he was a scorer against the Australians and bagged 15 tries in 22 games, as Halifax gained promotion. Injury again struck, however, keeping him out of Halifax's run to the Second Division Premiership final at Old Trafford.

# Peter Goodchild
Right-winger, 1966-1979

**Previous club:** Doncaster (1), Bramley (2)

**Halifax debut:** 17 December 1966 v. Hull Kingston Rovers

**Final Halifax appearance:** 11 March 1979 v. Swinton

**Appearances:** 128 + 2 subs

**Tries:** 51    **Goals:** 0    **Points:** 153

**Transferred to:** Bramley (1), retired (2)

**Honours:** Yorkshire

Peter Goodchild enjoyed an extraordinarily long career in professional rugby league, which took in over 500 appearances and stretched from 1961 to 1979. In all that time he played 14 games at centre but retained the pace and trickery, which allowed him to play the other 490-odd games at wing, a testimony to his enthusiasm and fitness.

After playing as an amateur for Hawksworth Old Boys, Peter joined Doncaster, a club then firmly rooted at the bottom of the league. In 175 games for them he scored 57 tries, a remarkable tally in the circumstances. Even more remarkable was the fact that Yorkshire selected him twice in 1966 despite Doncaster's ultra-low profile. Halifax realised what a fine winger he was – extremely quick with a splendid swerve and sidestep, which took him on amazing jinking runs to outstanding scores. He was a reliable defender too and Halifax paid £2,500 for his services.

At Thrum Hall he became a crowd favourite, scoring on his debut and running in several hat-tricks. One of his most notable feats was to score four tries at Dewsbury in 1968 but still to finish on the losing side, a very rare occurrence. In 1968/69, playing outside Welsh centre David Jones, he topped the Halifax try-scorers with 19 and played more games than anyone else (38). The nearest Halifax came to winning anything in his time at the club was a semi-final appearance in the Yorkshire Cup in 1968 but Peter did win a further Yorkshire cap in 1967,

when he bagged two tries in a 34-23 win over Cumberland at Castleford, his centre partner being former Thrum Haller Dave Stockwell.

In 1970 a £400 transfer took him to Bramley, for whom he scored two tries on his debut – a 17-5 victory over Halifax! Peter put in seven years of good service at Bramley, running in 66 tries in 199 games. In 1973/74 he scored an obstruction try in their historic victory over Widnes in the BBC2 Floodlit Trophy final and helped the club to promotion in 1976/77.

A final move brought Peter back to Halifax, for whom he made his second debut in an 11-12 defeat at Blackpool Borough on 29 January 1978. Halifax were at rock bottom in this period and Peter helped stabilise the team under coach Maurice Bamford, who arrived at Thrum Hall a month after Peter. On 30 September 1978 he scored his fiftieth try for Halifax, appropriately enough in a 16-0 home victory over his old club Bramley. He thus became one of a select band of players to have scored fifty tries for three different clubs. That band includes such luminaries as Ellery Hanley, Eric Batten, Terry Hollindrake and Phil Ford. He also joined another select group by playing at top level after his fortieth birthday. In 1976 Peter was jointly accorded the Yorkshire Federation Best and Fairest Player award with John Newlove.

# Harry Greenwood
Second-row forward, 1946-1953

**Previous club:** Ovenden ARL

**Halifax debut:** 28 December 1946 v. York

**Final Halifax appearance:** 9 May 1953
v. St Helens Championship final

**Appearances:** 131

**Tries:** 17    **Goals:** 0    **Points:** 51

**Transferred to:** Batley

Fans and players alike had a soft spot for Harry Greenwood, a local signed from Ovenden. Stan Kielty said, 'Harry was always cheerful. It was like a ray of sunshine in the dressing-room when Harry came in. He was one of those players for whom the game was about fun rather than money. People really liked him.'

Harry gave Halifax seven years of good service, most of which were not years of plenty at Thrum Hall. A six-footer and fourteen stones, fair-haired Harry was a pacey, strong-running, strong-tackling second-rower, who played the game as it should be played. He made his debut at loose forward in a 3-10 loss at York but played 112 of his 131 games in the second row with a variety of partners, the most notable being Charlie Smith in his early days and later Les White.

In 1948/49 Halifax reached Wembley but Harry did not figure in the Challenge Cup-ties. The following season he was firmly ensconced in the second row when Halifax surprised the critics by reaching the Championship semi-finals, losing to Wigan in a replay at Thrum Hall before a crowd of

28,150. Harry finished the season as the leading forward try-scorer with 9 in 30 games.

Harry played in 32 games in 1950/51, when he formed a mighty second-row pairing with Les White but fell down the pecking order in the next two seasons, appearing in the first team only six times. He did, however, pick up winners' medals in the Reserves, who won the Yorkshire Senior Competition Challenge Cup in 1951/52 and 1952/53.

By the end of the 1952/53 campaign Harry had played only one first-team game – a first-round Yorkshire Cup-tie at Bramley. He certainly was not expecting a recall for the Championship final clash with St Helens on 9 May 1953, but when Les White withdrew injured he was drafted in to the second row alongside Albert Fearnley. Halifax gave Saints a hard game but went down 14-24. For Harry it was the last game of his Halifax career and it was certainly one of his finest.

*The Rugby Leaguer* wrote, 'The star of the pack was undoubtedly Greenwood. The way he swept through the Saints ranks in the first half, to be stopped by Moses when all seemed lost for the Knowsley Road men, had an international look about it, and there were other occasions when he got away to figure in handling movements. It was indeed puzzling to learn that he was only a reserve.'

Harry, who died in 1999, had two sons who also played for Halifax, Lee and Brett. Both played for Halifax RU and Yorkshire. Lee, a centre, captained Halifax in 1976, and made 66 appearances for the club. Brett, a second-rower, made 41 appearances. His grandson, Brandon (winger) also played once in 1996.

# Tuss Griffiths
### Full-back, 1952-1956

**Previous club:** Doncaster

**Halifax debut:** 20 December 1952 *v.* Keighley

**Final Halifax appearance:** 8 September 1956
   *v.* Featherstone Rovers

**Appearances:** 151

**Tries:** 5  **Goals:** 438  **Points:** 891

**Transferred to:** Dewsbury

**Honours:** Wales

Tyssul 'Tuss' Griffiths was a full-back of the old school – a goal-kicker and field-kicker of considerable skill, who was cool under pressure, a good fielder of the ball and a man whose sound judgement in positioning compensated for a lack of genuine pace. His goal-kicking made him a match-winner and a record-breaker.

Six feet tall and thirteen stones, dark hair parted down the middle, Tuss always looked immaculate on the field. His career as a rugby union player began with Newport during the Second World War. In 1945/46 he played in the Monmouthshire XV which beat the New Zealand Services and won a Welsh 'Victory' cap against Scotland at Murrayfield, but within a month he signed for Hunslet.

Within six months he had won a Wales RL cap. Five years at Parkside was followed by a transfer to the new Doncaster club, where he gained another cap. Tuss remains the only Doncaster international player.

A fee of £850 brought him to Halifax in 1952, his two goals on his debut allowing Halifax to draw 4-4 at Keighley. On 21 March 1953 he landed nine goals in a 27-8 home victory over Dewsbury to establish a new post-war club record and landed four in Halifax's 14-24 loss to St Helens in the 1953 Championship final. A Yorkshire League winners' medal brought some consolation. In 1953/54 Tuss equalled Hubert Lockwood's club records of 117 goals and 237 points set back in 1937/38. He won another Yorkshire League medal but would have traded any one

of the myriad goals he had kicked for the late unsuccessful shot at goal he attempted against Warrington at Wembley in 1954, having landed two to give Halifax a 4-4 draw. He also kicked two each in the Odsal Replay and the Championship final but ultimately had to settle for runners-up medals.

In 1954/55 Tuss took over the captaincy briefly from Alvin Ackerley. He earned a Yorkshire Cup winners' medal that season, landing a record-equalling five goals in the final against Hull. The 1955/56 season brought him more winners' medals for the Yorkshire Cup and League but his goal against St Helens at Wembley provided Halifax's only points in a 2-13 defeat and the following week he was missing, because of a broken cheekbone, from the team which lost 9-10 to Hull in the Championship final. It was a fatal blow for Halifax failed to land any goals. Tuss would surely have kicked at least one and Halifax may have been champions. He had already shattered the club records in amassing 147 goals and 297 points. Uniquely, he simultaneously held the goal-kicking records at two clubs, having set a record for Doncaster with 89 goals in 1951/52. His consistency was exemplified in the statistic that he kicked goals in his last fifty-seven games for Halifax.

**Previous club:** Canterbury-Bankstown (1),
Newcastle Knights (2)

**Halifax debut:** 14 October 1984 v. Leigh

**Final Halifax appearance:** 7 May 1995
v. St Helens

**Appearances:** 92

**Tries:** 30    **Goals:** 1 drop goal    **Points:** 121

**Transferred to:** Retired

**Honours:** Queensland

Michael Hagan was the much younger brother of Bob Hagan, an Australian test centre, who played for Huddersfield from 1965 to 1967. Although Michael did not attain test status, he had a wonderful reputation in both hemispheres.

Michael was first graded with Canterbury-Bankstown in 1983 and came over to Halifax, aged twenty, in 1984. He immediately formed the most exciting half-back partnership Thrum Hall had seen for years with fellow Aussie Ron Ryan from Balmain. They simply ran opponents ragged. Nominally Michael was the scrum-half but both fed the scrums and it was difficult sometimes to work out who was playing where. Neither appeared a natural scrum-half, both being near six-footers, but they overrode their deficiencies by sheer talent, speed of thought and fleetness of foot.

Michael, then a trainee journalist, played twenty-five games in a row, helped Halifax to the semi-final of the John Player Trophy and finished as top try-scorer with 14, before returning home to play for Canterbury. He was runner-up to Martin Bella for the Player of the Year award despite his early departure.

Canterbury were a top club and in the next four years Michael played in three Grand Finals, winning two, figuring at stand-off in 1985, centre in 1986 and scrum-half in 1988. Among his teammates were former Halifax heroes Paul Langmack and Geoff Robinson.

Moving to Newcastle Knights in 1989, he made over 100 appearances in four years and was club captain. He played five State of Origin games for Queensland while a Knight.

Halifax fans were delighted to see Michael return to Thrum Hall in 1993, making his second debut in an 18-18 draw at Hull on 5 September. By then he had lost some pace but was an assured performer at stand-off. He was a tremendous organiser and ball-player, solid in defence and a shrewd reader of the game. The 1993/94 season brought him 33 uninterrupted appearances and 9 tries, as he struck up useful partnerships with scrum-halves Paul Bishop and Chris Robinson.

In 1994/95 Michael teamed up well with new scrum-half Wayne Parker and played in all 34 of Halifax's fixtures, scoring 7 tries and a solitary drop goal, in a 21-16 win at Hull. He also appeared against the Kangaroos, who won 26-12. Remarkably, in both his spells at Halifax he never missed a game, a testament to his fitness. He was a try-scorer in his last game for Halifax, a 16-32 defeat at St Helens.

Returning to Australia, Michael entered coaching and in his first year as a first-grade coach led Newcastle Knights to a 30-24 win over Parramatta in the 2001 Grand Final.

# Tony Halmshaw
Loose forward, 1966-1973

**Previous club:** Shaw Cross ARL

**Halifax debut:** 10 December 1966 v. Leeds

**Final Halifax appearance:** 18 March 1973 v. Doncaster

**Appearances:** 174 + 16 subs

**Tries:** 18   **Goals:** 8   **Points:** 70

**Transferred to:** Rochdale Hornets

**Honours:** Yorkshire, Great Britain

Tony Halmshaw was fourth in a distinguished line of fair-haired international loose forwards who graced the blue and white jersey over a two decade period, following in the footsteps of Des Clarkson, Ken Traill and Charlie Renilson. Tony was not as fortunate as the other three in terms of the teams in which he played but he certainly made his mark. He was a skilful ball distributor, an astute tactical and touch kicker, a hard runner and stern tackler and he was a tough opponent, who kept going when others wilted.

Tony signed for Halifax on 17 June 1965 for a fee of £1,000 – a lot for a junior. He was one of a gaggle of Shaw Cross players, who signed around the same time but he was the only one to make the grade. With Charlie Renilson still ruling the roost Tony had to wait over a year for his first-team debut, a 5-11 home defeat by Leeds. Jackie Pycroft also made his debut and it was Duncan Jackson's last game for the club. He was, however, a star turn in the reserves, winning the 'A' team Player of the Year award in 1966/67.

By 1968/69 he had established a first-team place, Renilson moving forward to second row or prop. On 4 January 1969 Tony played full-back for the only time in a home game against Featherstone Rovers. His performances in 30 appearances had been good enough to win the first team Player of the Year award. In 1969/70 he was an ever-present with 39 appearances.

In 1970/71 Tony seemed to conjure up some extra pace to add to his repertoire and

was selected for Yorkshire, who routed Lancashire 34-8 at Castleford to lift the County Championship. He was again on the winning side, 42-22, and a try-scorer in the following Roses Match at Leigh on 29 September 1971, and earned a second County Championship winners' medal when Cumberland were beaten 17-12 at Wakefield. With Halifax he had a sensational season in 1971/72, starring in the series of ties which resulted in Halifax winning the inaugural John Player Trophy and reaching the Challenge Cup semi-final. He again won the Player of the Year award, emulating the great Colin Dixon in winning it twice. The test selectors also recognised his merit, capping him in the third test against New Zealand at Headingley, a game Britain won 12-3.

Elected captain for 1972/73 and capped again by Yorkshire, Tony scored the only hat-trick of his career in a 76-8 victory at Hunslet in the first round of the Yorkshire Cup. He led Halifax to the semi-finals of the Yorkshire Cup but Halifax went out in the first round to St Helens in the John Player Trophy and to Warrington in the Challenge Cup, both highly contentious games. Disillusioned by the decline of the club, he was transferred to Rochdale Hornets for £5,000.

Open-side prop, 1991-1998

**Previous club:** Hull

**Halifax debut:** 1 September 1991 v.
Featherstone Rovers

**Final Halifax appearance:** 9 October 1998
v. St Helens

**Appearances:** 199 + 4

**Tries:** 13    **Goals:** 0    **Points:** 52

**Transferred to:** Hull

**Honours:** England, Great Britain

Karl 'Rhino' Harrison can boast two unique distinctions as a Halifax player, which marks him out as a very special player in the club's long history. Firstly, he is Halifax's most capped Great Britain Test player, having won 11 of his 14 caps while a Thrum Haller, superseding the record of another great prop, Ken Roberts, who gained 10. Secondly, he is the longest serving captain in the club's existence. Karl skippered Halifax for the last six years of his eight season career at Halifax (1993/94 through to 1998), having also captained the side for most of the 1992/93 season. Alfred Walsh, who captained Halifax in their first five seasons (1873/74 to 1877/78), had previously held the captaincy record for consecutive seasons. Karl's longevity of leadership exceeded that of such notable skippers as James Dodd, Joe Riley, Dai Rees, Hubert Lockwood, Alvin Ackerley and John Burnett, all revered figures in the pantheon of Fax captains.

Born in Morley in 1964, Karl played schools rugby union for Morley High School and league for Drighlington as a junior. He eventually ended up as a back-rower with BRK Gildersome before joining Bramley Colts when Maurice Bamford was in charge. Karl's signing-on fee for Bramley was £250 in

January 1983. When he left, after three years and 82 games, his value had rocketed to £15,000, a club record for Featherstone Rovers. Karl gave Rovers three and a half seasons service (114 games), helped them to promotion in 1987/88 and appeared in their Second Division Premiership defeat by Oldham at Old Trafford.

Karl had been transformed from a fearsome second-rower into a top-notch prop in his days at Post Office Road and ambitious Hull were prepared to expend £57,000 for his signature in August 1989. Two seasons with the Airlie Birds brought him test recognition and a Premiership winners' medal, when Hull famously beat favourites Widnes 14-4 at Old Trafford in 1991. That proved to be Karl's last game for Hull, however, for he became Halifax's first £100,000 capture when he moved to Thrum Hall for the start of 1991/92.

Even at that vast price Karl may be considered a bargain for he became the absolute mainstay of Halifax's pack for most of the 1990s. Moustachioed and massive, Karl weighed in at over seventeen stones and stood about 6' 3". In style he was not spectacular but he had a profound influence on the team. Everyone knew that he would be going just as strongly at the end of a game as at the start, his weight and power taking the steam out of the opposing pack. He was both worker and leader. On the rare occasions when he was absent he was sorely missed and whenever he was substituted in his latter days, there seemed

*Karl Harrison prepares to take on the Leeds defence.*

to be a drop in the pack's intensity. Karl rarely had a bad game, while his cajoling of his side and relentless play were inspirational. Although Karl had come through the game in the days of competitive scrummaging, the five-metre rule and contested play-the-balls, he adapted well to the changing game of the late twentieth century.

Halifax had gained promotion in 1990/91 and while no tangible rewards were won under Karl, there were plenty of interesting times and the club held a respectable position in the top flight. In his first season Karl missed one game and in his second, 1992/93, he was an ever-present in 33 fixtures. He took over the captaincy at the start of the season, relinquished it briefly to fellow prop John Fieldhouse but was in charge in one of Halifax's most dramatic games when a last-gasp Joe Lydon drop goal robbed the blue and whites of a Challenge Cup semi-final, Wigan beating them 19-18 at Thrum Hall in a snowstorm. Never a prolific try-scorer, Karl had his best return (4) for the club in 1992/93.

In 1994 Karl captained Halifax in their 12-26 defeat by the Australians, was in charge through the Rugby League Centenary season and when the game entered the Super League era. In 1997 he led Halifax in their encounters with Brisbane, Canberra and Canterbury in the ill-fated World Club Challenge, as Halifax endured a poor campaign. On 22 March 1998 Karl played against Leeds in Halifax's last match at Thrum Hall, a 35-28 win, and led them to a 30-6 victory over Huddersfield in their first game at The Shay. That season was to be his swansong with Halifax, whom he led to third place in Super League, a tremendous achievement, only five of twenty-three matches being lost.

Unaccountably, Halifax decided to dispense with their captain's services at that point, leaving a bad taste in everyone's mouths. Karl had not wanted to leave and the fans certainly did not want him to go. Hindsight reinforces the contemporary view that his departure was calamitous.

In representative football Karl gained a reputation commensurate with his huge physique. He never played in a Challenge Cup final at Wembley but did appear there three times for Great Britain, winning each time. He made his Test debut there in a brilliant 19-12 win against Australia in 1990, was in the side that beat New Zealand 17-0 in 1993 and figured in the heroic one-man-short team which beat the Aussies 8-4 in 1994. Another triumph was the Lions' devastating 33-10 defeat of Australia at Melbourne in 1992. He also won 6 England caps.

# John Henderson

Second-row forward, prop, 1955-1958

**Previous club:** Workington Town

**Halifax debut:** 5 February 1955 v. Warrington

**Final Halifax appearance:** 18 January 1958
    v. Hull Kingston Rovers

**Appearances:** 90

**Tries:** 6   **Goals:** 0   **Points:** 18

**Transferred to:** York

**Honours:** Cumberland, England, Great Britain

John Henderson was one of many Cumbrians to have played successfully with Halifax. Born in Maryport in 1929, John made his reputation with Workington Town, playing 107 games for them between 1950 and 1954. Town won the Championship in 1950/51 and the Challenge Cup in 1951/52, although he played in neither final. His performances were good enough, however, to gain him his Cumberland debut in 1952 and an England cap against Wales in 1953. In 1954 he went to Australia and New Zealand as a Lion on one of the most controversial tours in history.

Halifax signed John for £2,000 before the Challenge Cup register closed in 1955. They bought an experienced, no-nonsense forward, a real grafter, prepared to do the hard work and expend all of his energy. A solid force at 5' 10.5" and fifteen stones, John embodied all the characteristics of a typical Cumbrian forward – hard, powerful, unrelenting and rugged.

John played his first couple of games at blind-side prop for Halifax but was more usually employed in the second row, forming a dangerous combination with Derrick Schofield in those early days. Never a great try-scorer, he scored his first in the last league fixture of the season in a 26-7 victory at Doncaster, just two days before Halifax were beaten at Warrington

in the Championship semi-finals. That game at Wilderspool was 'Fax's eleventh in twenty-five days and John played in every one, along with other iron-men forwards, Alvin Ackerley, Jack Wilkinson and Schofield.

Season 1955/56 was the most momentous in John's career. He played at blind-side prop in Halifax's 18-17 defeat of the New Zealanders but was in the second row six weeks later for the Yorkshire Cup final at Headingley against Hull. He scored the opening try but was sent off on the hour in almost riotous circumstances. The game was drawn 10-10 and John was suspended for the replay which Halifax won 7-0. He had his winners' medal, however, and added a Yorkshire League winners' medal too.

The 1955/56 season saw him pick up runners-up medals for the Challenge Cup, when he played at prop against St Helens at Wembley, and for the Championship, when he was in the second row against Hull at Maine Road. The following season brought him an appearance at blind-side prop in Halifax's 6-3 victory over the Kangaroos and a trip to France with Halifax, who won 19-11 in Albi and 24-9 in Carcassonne in the European Club Championship with John in the second row both times. Later in the season he played hooker for the only time at Wigan.

1957/58 was his last at Thrum Hall and he played enough games to get another Yorkshire League Championship-winners' medal. He also won the last two of his eight Cumberland caps before joining York for £2,700.

# Tony Hepworth
### Utility back, 1967-1976

**Previous club:** Shaw Cross ARL

**Halifax debut:** 19 August 1967 v. Hull
Kingston Rovers

**Final Halifax appearance:** 15 February 1976
v. Keighley  Challenge Cup

**Appearances:** 218 + 12 subs

**Tries:** 66   **Goals:** 0   **Points:** 198

**Transferred to:** Retired

Born in Heckmondwike in 1947, Tony Hepworth was a gifted player – a good handler, a deceptive and elusive attacking player, sound in defence and a man with a try-scoring instinct. He was solidly built too at six feet and fourteen stones. Above all, however, he was one of the most versatile backs to have played for Halifax in the post-war period. His record shows that he started at full-back on 90 occasions, right-wing (1), right-centre (27), left-centre (35), left-wing (30) and stand-off (35) but often played in several positions in one game. He was a very useful player for any coach to have in a squad.

Signed from Shaw Cross, Dewsbury for £750 in 1967, he began his first-team career aged nineteen, playing at right-centre to Peter Goodchild. In his sixth game he scored a hat-trick in a 27-18 home victory over Salford on 8 September 1967 and bagged 12 tries in 19 games in his debut season. On 13 April 1968 against Hull KR at Thrum Hall he performed a possibly unique feat for Halifax by scoring a hat-trick after substituting for Goodchild on the right-wing at half-time.

For the next couple of years Halifax appeared not to know where to play Tony, who seemed to slot in wherever he was required. Many thought his best position was at centre, where he often played well in combination with David Jones.

By 1970 he had played everywhere in the backs except scrum-half but was employed mainly at left wing outside David Willicombe in 1970/71, when he was top try-scorer with 16, including four in a 41-10 win at Blackpool

Borough. In 1971/72 he was thrust into the full-back role when Ronnie James was injured at Wakefield Trinity and took to it like a duck to water. Ronnie never got back in the team and Tony was a revelation as Halifax won the John Player Trophy and reached the Challenge Cup semi-final. Tony scored the only try in Halifax's heart-stopping 9-8 third-round victory over Swinton and was the only try-scorer when they lost 3-16 to Leeds in the semi-final at Odsal. During that season Tony played a staggering 45 games out of 47.

The following season saw Tony set a new club record, scoring 12 tries from full-back – Ronnie James was the previous holder with 8 in 1963/64. He also became the first Thrum Haller to score a hat-trick from full-back – in Halifax's record 76-8 victory at Hunslet in the first round of the Yorkshire Cup – and the first Halifax full-back to register tries in four consecutive matches – against Barrow, Hunslet, Castleford and Wakefield Trinity during August and September 1972.

Injuries spoiled the latter part of Tony's career as the team which won the John Player Trophy disintegrated, culminating in relegation in 1974/75.

# Brendan Hill
Prop, 1989-1993

**Previous club:** Bradford Northern

**Halifax debut:** 15 January 1989 v. Wigan

**Final Halifax appearance:** 23 April 1993
v. St Helens

**Appearances:** 73 + 21 subs

**Tries:** 23 **Goals:** 0 **Points:** 92

**Transferred to:** Keighley Cougars

**Honours:** Yorkshire, Great Britain Under-21s

Brendan Hill was one of the most awesome sights in rugby league from the mid-1980s to the mid-1990s. A massive barrel of a man, Brendan brought crowds to their feet, opponents to their knees and some coaches to despair. Despite his bulk, Brendan was remarkably agile and quicker than given credit for. He was tremendously difficult to stop and it was one of the great spectacles of the game to see two, three and four tacklers piling into him but unable to prevent him from popping out the sweetest of passes to a colleague. That took real skill and nerve.

Naturally, opponents were obsessed with stopping him, and they were also worried about being tackled by him. Consequently, he was a great distraction to opposing packs and a boon to his own team. In the days of competitive scrummaging – the first half of his career – he was indispensable and seemed to be able to shove the opposing scrum backwards on his own. Apart from his sheer physicality, Brendan was a good footballer, who scored 68 tries in his career at a try every four games, a remarkable figure for a prop.

Brendan began as an amateur with Queensbury and signed for Leeds in 1982, where he won Yorkshire Colts honours and

represented Great Britain Under-21s against France and Yorkshire against Lancashire. A £30,000 move to Bradford Northern followed in 1986. While at Odsal he was awarded the Man of the Match award for his display in their Yorkshire Cup final replay victory over Castleford in 1987, when the official programme listed his weight as 18st 4lb.

Halifax signed Brendan for £90,000 on 11 January 1989, the fee being the largest to date for a specialist prop. His debut at Wigan coincided with that of second-rower Paul Medley, another big-money signing. Brendan arrived too late in the season to prevent Halifax being relegated. He scored his first try for the club in the last game of the season, a 40-8 demolition of St Helens.

Brendan proved a firm favourite of the Thrum Hall fans. In 1989/90 Halifax reached the Yorkshire Cup semi-final and contested the Regal Trophy final, when Brendan scored Halifax's only try in a 12-24 loss to Wigan at Headingley. His season's tally was 9, six of which came in a late four-match spell. Season 1990/91 saw him claim 11 tries in 32 games. He gave a rousing performance against the Kangaroos and late in the season took over the captaincy. Halifax won promotion and Brendan scored a try in their 20-27 defeat by Salford in the Second Division Premiership final at Old Trafford.

He fell out of favour under coach Roger Millward, making only 21 appearances in two seasons and losing his open-side berth to Karl Harrison. However, reserve-team crowds rose!

# Granville Hoyle

Second-row forward, 1973-1976

**Previous club:** Swinton

**Halifax debut:** 25 November 1973 v. Batley

**Final Halifax appearance:** 7 November 1976 v. Blackpool Borough John Player Trophy

**Appearances:** 93

**Tries:** 37 **Goals:** 0 **Points:** 111

**Transferred to:** Rochdale Hornets

Halifax have had few more spectacular running forwards than Granville Hoyle, who was a real favourite with Thrum Hall crowds. Granville was 6' 1" and weighed over sixteen stones but he could run faster than most backs and a lot more damagingly. He scored exhilarating tries from his own half through sheer pace and power and he scored tries from a few yards out because he could spot the weak point of defences and was quick to exploit them. Granville was a genuine crowd-pleaser and match-winner. It was such a shame he did not play in a better Halifax team.

A native of Huddersfield, Granville played as an amateur for the local St Joseph's team before signing for Swinton, where he spent seven years. His only major final in the game was Swinton's 11-25 loss to Salford in the 1972 Lancashire Cup final. Halifax signed him for £2,000 in November 1973 and he was an immediate hit. He scored a try after seven minutes of his debut and then made another for Graham Pitchforth. Thereafter the fans expected fireworks every time he played and usually got them, for he illuminated many of the matches in which he figured.

In his first season, 1973/74, Halifax scraped a promotion place when they finished fourth, Granville contributing 10 tries in 21 games. He made history on 27 January 1974 when he scored the first seven-point try at Thrum Hall after being fouled by New Hunslet's hooker as he touched down in the sixty-seventh minute. The try won the game 14-12.

In 1974/75 Halifax were relegated but Granville continued to scintillate. He was joint top try-scorer with Bruce Burton on 12 in 33 appearances. He created more records by becoming the first Halifax forward to score ten or more tries in consecutive seasons since the formation of the Northern Union. In scoring a hat-trick on 30 March 1975 in an 18-28 defeat at Dewsbury, he became the first Halifax forward to have ever done so in a loss. A staggering try in a Floodlit Trophy tie against Hull KR provoked Rovers into making a very large offer for him which was rejected.

The 1975/76 campaign brought 9 tries in 28 games as Halifax continued to nosedive. Granville played on into 1976/77 clocking up another 6 tries in 11 appearances. He played on the wing in a 20-3 win at Whitehaven and scored three tries in a 24-4 victory against Ovenden in a John Player Trophy tie from right-centre. However, he never played for the club again after being substituted at half-time in a disastrous 3-7 defeat at Blackpool Borough in the second round of the John Player Trophy. A fee of £2,500 was obtained on his transfer to Rochdale but that was scant consolation for the distraught 'Fax fans.

# Duncan Jackson
Right-winger, 1959-1966

**Previous club:** Headingley RU

**Halifax debut:** 14 March 1959 v. Doncaster

**Final Halifax appearance:** 10 December 1966
    v. Leeds

**Appearances:** 121 + 1 sub

**Tries:** 76   **Goals:** 0   **Points:** 228

**Transferred to:** Retired

**Honours:** Yorkshire

Halifax signed Duncan Jackson in 1957 when he was a sixteen-year-old rugby union winger. A £1,500 fee was indicative that he was regarded as special. Duncan made his debut, aged seventeen years and nine months, in the first team at Doncaster sixteen months later, scoring twice in a 32-16 win. There was no rush to get him in the first team, as Alan Snowden, Keith Williams and Johnny Freeman were available for the wing. Duncan played in the reserves for four years, rattling up 105 tries, with 32 in 1959/60 his best.

Those four years also brought him 14 tries in 18 first-team outings, including a first hat-trick against Hunslet on 4 April 1962. The next three years brought him a permanent place in the firsts and a fine collection of winners' medals in major competitions. Duncan proved a very competent performer on Halifax's right wing. He was especially dependable on defence, coach Albert Fearnley regarding his combination with centre John Burnett as a big contributory factor to the team's triumphs. As an attacking player he had considerable pace, was a good finisher and had a happy and useful knack of snapping up tries in big games.

In 1962/63, his first full season, Duncan helped Halifax reach the semi-finals of the Yorkshire Cup and Eastern Division Championship, scored a notable seventy-yard runaway try against Leeds at Headingley to beat Leeds 5-3, and finished with 14 tries in 31 appearances.

The 1963/64 season was even better as Duncan shared the leading try-scorer's title with Johnny Freeman on 22. In the Yorkshire Cup final, a 10-0 victory over Featherstone at Wakefield, Duncan supported an interception from Burnett to score Halifax's first try. He was at it again when Halifax also lifted the Eastern Division Championship at the end of the campaign, scoring twice in the semi-final against Wakefield Trinity and adding another pair of opportunistic tries in the final at Fartown, where Castleford were beaten 20-12.

The following season yielded Duncan 20 tries in 31 matches. Yet again he proved his mettle on the big occasions. At Swinton in the Championship final Halifax were struggling to hold a 10-7 lead over St Helens with just minutes remaining, when Duncan bagged the try which clinched the Championship after great play by Fogerty, Robinson and Daley.

Sadly, he played only another dozen games for Halifax. After scoring against the New Zealanders at Thrum Hall on 28 August 1965 injury kept him out for over a year. Despite recovering, further knee problems caused him to retire before he turned twenty-seven.

In 1962 Duncan represented Yorkshire twice, gaining a County Championship-winners' medal. He won a third cap against Cumberland in 1964. All his county caps were won as a left-winger, partnering Neil Fox, and he was always on the winning side.

# Neil James
Second-row forward, 1985-1990

**Previous club:** Castleford

**Halifax debut:** 1 September 1985 v. Oldham

**Final Halifax appearance:** 4 April 1990 v. Hull Kingston Rovers

**Appearances:** 98 + 24 subs

**Tries:** 19   **Goals:** 0   **Points:** 76

**Transferred to:** Leeds

**Honours:** Great Britain

When Neil James arrived at Thrum Hall on loan from Castleford in August 1985, his career appeared to have stalled, as he had fallen out of favour with coach Mal Reilly. He had been a junior of promise, figuring in the BARLA Great Britain Test team which lost 14-19 against France in 1978/79. He had played 111 games for Castleford, scoring 17 tries and numbered among his appearances was the Yorkshire Cup final of 1983, when Hull had triumphed 13-2 at Elland Road.

Neil's loan to Halifax dragged on into October 1985 and he had already played 9 games before his signing was completed. It was finally agreed that Alan Shillito and £5,000 would go to Wheldon Road in exchange. Neil had all the physical qualities required for a top-class second-rower. He stood six feet tall and weighed fifteen stones and he could certainly shift. He fitted well into the great pack which Chris Anderson had put together and which was the platform for Halifax's drive to the Championship in Neil's first season as a blue and white. Neil formed a fine second-row partnership with Mick Scott, contributing 34 appearances (4 tries) during 1985/86. He appeared in the Premiership final against Warrington but had perhaps his greatest game for Halifax at Headingley in a league fixture when Halifax won 22-20, their first league victory at Leeds in twenty-two years. He was practically unstoppable that afternoon.

His form was so good that he became Halifax's first test player for eleven years –

since David Willicombe in 1974 – when Maurice Bamford selected him to play against France at Wigan on 1 March 1986. Neil scored a try in a 24-10 victory and won the Man of the Match award.

In 1986/87 Neil made 33 appearances, 14 of which were as a substitute, as the second-row spots rotated between Scott, Paul Dixon, Brian Juliff and himself. It was another fantastic campaign. Neil played in the Charity Shield victory over his old team Castleford on the Isle of Man and played as a substitute in the Wembley victory over St Helens.

In 1987/88 Neil played in the Charity Shield loss against Wigan and at Wembley, where Wigan again beat Halifax, scoring one of his side's two tries. On 1 January 1988 Neil switched to bind-side prop against Swinton and remained there for the rest of the season.

The following two seasons brought him only 27 appearances as Halifax fell from the First Division. On 28 August 1988 Neil scored a hat-trick from the second-row in a 26-20 home win against Widnes but missed most of the rest of the season. In 1990 he went on loan to Leeds and eventually signed for them and subsequently went to Sheffield Eagles. In October 1993 Neil was loaned to Halifax from Sheffield but did not appear in the first team.

# Ronnie James
Full-back, 1961-1971

**Previous club:** Maesteg RU

**Halifax debut:** 25 March 1961 v. Batley

**Final Halifax appearance:** 14 November 1971 v. Warrington John Player Trophy

**Appearances:** 371 + 1 sub

**Tries:** 45   **Goals:** 1,028   **Points:** 2,191

**Transferred to:** Retired

**Honours:** Commonwealth XIII

Very few players kick 1,000 goals for one club. Ronnie James is the only Halifax player ever to have achieved that target and his nearest challenger, the great Hubert Lockwood, landed only 819. Ronnie also holds the club record for points scored – 2,191 – and is the only Halifax player to have reached a century of goals in a season four times.

Despite such impressive statistics, many fans will remember Ronnie more for the fun and excitement he brought to Thrum Hall in the way he transformed full-back play. Previous 'Fax full-backs had generally fallen into the old classic mould – safe catchers, sound tacklers, long field-kickers, ultra-reliable positional players. There had been a long line of such men, fine practitioners, going right back to Alf Chorley at the dawn of the Northern Union. Billy Little, Willie Metcalfe, Clem Garforth, Dick Davies, Hubert Lockwood, Dennis Chalkley, Tuss Griffiths and Garfield Owen represented a gifted collection of players who had worn the number one jersey for the blue and whites.

Ronnie was good at the things they were good at, of course, but he was also mad keen to attack. He was tremendous at running through defences, scattering defenders after fielding kicks and his try tally of 45 tries, all from full-back, was far more than all the other full-backs in the post-war period (1945/60) had gathered between them. His best haul of 8 tries in 1963/64 established a club record for

a full-back, subsequently beaten by Tony Hepworth and some of the more recent full-backs playing under changed circumstances. When Ronnie was brought to ground, his efforts to quickly play the ball, so common nowadays, caused consternation to defenders, who often conceded penalties for holding him down. There tended to be bodies all over the place. The fans loved his enthusiasm.

Although he was not a big man at about 5' 8", Ronnie weighed around thirteen stones, had tree-trunk legs and was tremendously powerful. He was a long touch-finder and a prolific dropper of goals in an era when drop-kicking was unusual. His goal-kicking was spectacularly good, and occasionally erratic. A thousand goals, however, represents exceptional kicking at any level.

Ronnie came north from Wales in 1959. He had played for his native village Ystalyfera and Maesteg as a union player and had had a few games for Swansea. Halifax's contract was worth £1,250 to him, with £750 of it on signature. It was money well spent. Even so, it took Ronnie two years to gain a first-team place and there was great controversy when Halifax decided to play Ronnie at full-back in preference to the popular Garfield Owen. Once in the team, however, Ronnie spent the next decade there, shattering records and entertaining the Thrum Hall faithful.

In 1961/62, his first full season, he scored 160 points but far exceeded that the following season, when he played in all 44 of the club's fixtures, piling up 261 points (123 goals, 5 tries).

*A murky day at Thrum Hall in 1966 and Ronnie James crashes over for a try against Bramley. David Jones celebrates. Winger John Simpson and Terry Ramshaw can also be seen.*

In 1963/64 he again topped the century with 105 goals and failed to land a goal only once in 38 appearances – in the 0-3 home defeat by Batley in the Cup – when he broke his foot. Ronnie picked up his first winners' medals that season, landing two goals in the Yorkshire Cup final defeat of Featherstone and four when Castleford were beaten in the Eastern Division Championship final.

Halifax stormed to the Championship in 1964/65, Ronnie converting all three tries in the 15-7 Championship final triumph over St Helens at Swinton. It proved his best scoring season, as he claimed 268 points (125 goals, 6 tries) in 40 outings. He equalled the club post-war record with nine goals in a 51-0 home thrashing of Doncaster.

Although Halifax again reached the Championship final in 1965/66, Ronnie was out injured. Despite missing the last eleven games of the campaign, he had scored 186 points (90 goals, 2 tries) and won his solitary representative honour, an appearance for a Commonwealth XIII against New Zealand at Crystal Palace. He was unfortunate to play the game at a time when rugby league had abandoned Wales as an international XIII.

In 1966/67 Ronnie had put up some wonderful displays in a Halifax team which was beginning to struggle. Included was a magnificent eight from eight goal tally in a 34-22 win at Wigan. In 25 games he rattled up 185 points before dropping a bombshell by announcing his retirement on 10 February 1967. Fortunately, he changed his mind and returned for the final game of the season and went on for another five years.

The last half-decade of his career brought little success to Halifax but there were highlights for Ronnie. He played in the Wigan Sevens-winning side of 1967 and appeared in Halifax's game against the 1967 Kangaroos, while in 1968/69 he took over the captaincy when Colin Dixon was transferred. That 1968/69 season was the last time he kicked a century of goals – 113, fifteen of which were dropped. In 1970/71 he fell just four goals short of a fifth century but had the satisfaction of establishing a post-war record in booting ten goals in a 47-15 crushing of Bramley at Thrum Hall. His consistency was rewarded with the Player of the Year award.

Ronnie seemed to be playing as well as ever in 1971/72, kicking 50 goals in 15 appearances, but retired after a substitute appearance at Warrington in the first round of the new John Player Trophy competition. Injuries had taken their toll on Halifax's most prolific scorer but he continued to play locally with Mixenden and Queensbury.

# David Jones
Centre, winger, 1966-1971

**Previous club:** Maesteg RU

**Halifax debut:** 1 January 1966 v. Featherstone Rovers

**Final Halifax appearance:** 25 April 1971 v. Salford

**Appearances:** 199 + 3 subs

**Tries:** 69   **Goals:** 10   **Points:** 227

**Transferred to:** Retired

**Honours:** Wales

Halifax had been luring Welsh centres north since 1891, when Cardiff's Bill Keepings arrived at Thrum Hall, ostensibly to further his career in boilermaking. Seventy-four years later he was followed by Neath-born metallurgist David Jones, who had attracted Halifax's attention with some spectacular performances for Maesteg. Following a trial against Doncaster 'A', which was won 24-4, on 30 October 1965, he was signed for £2,000. At six feet and thirteen stones, the twenty-one-year-old three-quarter was soon in the first team, initially making his mark on the right wing, successfully filling the gap left by Duncan Jackson's injury and retirement. He played 21 games in his first season and scored a dozen tries, as Halifax confounded everyone by reaching the Championship final from tenth position in the league. David played in all the Championship play-off games, earning the only medal of his career, albeit a runners-up, as St Helens hammered Halifax 35-12 in the final at Swinton. The nearest Halifax came to further glory in David's time was limited to appearances in the semi-finals of the Yorkshire Cup in 1966 and 1968.

In the following two seasons David topped the Halifax try-scorers lists, with 17 in 1966/67 and 16 in 1967/68, pipping Colin Dixon on both occasions. In 1967/68 he shared the club Player of the Year award with

Charlie Renilson. By then he was well established as the right-centre, having pace and determination, while his high knee action made him particularly awkward to tackle.

During his sojourn at Thrum Hall David struck up a fruitful centre-wing partnership with Peter Goodchild, helping the winger to 19 tries in 1968/69, and he was always a popular player with the fans. In 1967 he played against the Kangaroos but Halifax were defeated 22-2 and would not meet the Australians again until 1986.

Although a consistent try-scorer, it was not until 18 April 1971 that he scored his only hat-trick for the club in a 45-17 rout of Doncaster at Tattersfield – his 201st game. The following week he played his last game for Halifax in a 3-33 loss at Salford.

Remarkably, ten years later, aged around thirty-six, he re-emerged in Cardiff City Blue Dragons' colours, making his debut against Halifax and scoring a try, as Halifax won 31-21 at Ninian Park on 11 October 1981. He also played, at full-back, in the return fixture at Thrum Hall on 21 March 1982, when Cardiff won 22-10.

David Jones was selected twice for Wales, making his international debut in a surprise 24-17 win against England at Salford on 7 November 1968, when, as left-centre, he partnered Clive Sullivan. On 18 October 1969 he reverted to right-centre, partnering Frank Wilson and scoring a try in a 23-40 loss to England at Headingley.

# Alan Kellett
Stand-off, centre, 1954-1971

**Previous club:** Oldham (1), Bradford Northern (2)

**Halifax debut:** 13 November 1954
*v.* Wakefield Trinity

**Final Halifax appearance:** 25 April 1971
*v.* Salford

**Appearances:** 125 + 3 subs

**Tries:** 23   **Goals:** 18   **Points:** 105

**Transferred to:** Bradford Northern (1), Oldham (2)

**Honours:** Yorkshire

Alan Kellett joined Halifax four times over a period of twenty-two years, which must be some sort of record for the club!

A local, Alan played as an amateur with Ovenden and was soon spotted as a likely future star. Halifax gave him trials as a seventeen-year-old in November 1954, when he played for the first team against Wakefield Trinity and Hunslet, scoring a try in the latter match at Thrum Hall. With Ken Dean in his pomp at stand-off, Halifax chose not to sign Alan who was quickly snapped up by Oldham.

Alan spent eight years at Watersheddings, learning his trade with one of the great teams of post-war rugby league. By 1958 he had established himself as Oldham's regular stand-off and developed an outstanding half-back combination with Frank Pitchford. Alan had blossomed into a superb try-scoring half-back. He was a member of the Lancashire League Championship-winning side in 1957/58 and he was in the Oldham side which beat St Helens 12-2 in the 1958 Lancashire Cup final, dropping a goal and getting a try. He played in Championship semi-finals in 1958 and 1959 and in the Challenge Cup semi-final in 1960, as well as appearing against the 1955 and 1961 Kiwis and the 1959 Kangaroos.

When Halifax signed Alan in August 1963, he was the finished article, a veteran of almost 200 games for Oldham in which he had amassed 76 tries and 4 goals. He had also won

6 caps for Yorkshire in which he had scored 6 tries, including a hat-trick against the 1959 Australians in a 47-15 victory at York. It was an abiding mystery to many critics that he had not won higher honours, although he had been selected in 'Shadow' test teams and was among the reserves for the 1960 World Cup.

Alan cost Halifax £4,500, a big fee. They got good value, however, and they certainly knew what they were buying, as Alan had many times been Halifax's downfall in games against the Roughyeds. In both the 1958/59 league clashes he had scored tries against Halifax, while in 1960/61 he had run them ragged with hat-tricks at Watersheddings (Oldham winning 17-15) and at Thrum Hall (Oldham winning 28-9). Together with another newcomer, forward Ken Roberts, Alan became one of the pivots of a team which was to restore former glories to Halifax.

By the time Alan arrived at Thrum Hall he had lost the searing pace of his best days at Oldham but made up for it in guile and nous. He was an astute playmaker, who knew the strengths and weaknesses of the opposition. He had great hands and a good boot on him and he was brave and tenacious as a defender, who never hid when things got tough. Much of the back play revolved around him and he rarely made significant errors.

Within months of his arrival Halifax had won the Yorkshire Cup. Alan had scored tries in the first two rounds against Keighley and Wakefield Trinity and had been a key man in

*Alan Kellett slices through during an 8-3 victory against Huddersfield at Thrum Hall on Christmas Day 1963.*

the 10-9 semi-final win at Dewsbury. Unfortunately, injury kept him out of the final. Until the latter part of the season Alan operated at stand-off but was moved to centre, allowing Barry Robinson to move to number six. The numbers on the pair's backs were often irrelevant as Alan was the fulcrum, particularly at set moves. He was at centre at Fartown where Halifax beat Castleford to win the Eastern Division Championship.

Alan's debut season at Halifax was a roaring success. He shared top billing in the appearances list on 39 with Ronnie James and Johnny Freeman and was Player of the Year.

The following season he was runner-up to Colin Dixon for Player of the Year, became vice-captain in January 1965 and was substitute for both Yorkshire matches. He played more matches than anyone else (41), claiming 12 tries and 12 goals, one of them a match-winning drop goal at Bradford, who were beaten 9-7. He scored a try hat-trick in a 51-0 win against Doncaster but was sent off, along with Don Fox, in a 4-24 loss at Featherstone Rovers. At the end of the season Alan moved from stand-off to left-centre, playing there in the play-off matches and in

Halifax's 15-7 victory over St Helens in the Championship final.

In 1965/66 Alan was in such good form that he represented Yorkshire against Cumberland at centre and at stand-off in victories over Lancashire, and the New Zealanders. His season was punctuated, however, by controversy. In October he was transfer listed at £8,000 but was appointed secretary at Bradford Northern within a month. Less than two weeks later he resigned and was back playing for Halifax. He came off the transfer list in March but was back on it in April and did not play again for Halifax, missing the run to the Championship final. He was transferred to Bradford in June 1966 for £1,250.

Alan then spent two spells at Odsal and periods with Keighley and Oldham. He came back to Thrum Hall for the third time in 1970, kicking a couple of goals on his return in an 11-4 victory at Keighley on 14 November and remaining until the end of the season, totalling 19 appearances (6 goals, 1 try). A varied coaching career (1968/86) took him to Keighley (three times), Bradford and Carlisle, and Halifax for 1976/77. His playing days ended as player-coach to Siddal.

# Stuart Kelley
Hooker, prop, 1962-1970

**Previous club:** Shaw Cross ARL

**Halifax debut:** 22 December 1962 v. Oldham

**Final Halifax appearance:** 18 April 1970
v. Leeds

**Appearances:** 136 + 8 subs

**Tries:** 10   **Goals:** 0   **Points:** 30

**Transferred to:** Wakefield Trinity

Combative, uncompromising, in-yer-face would be the type of descriptions for a player like Stuart Kelley in modern times. He was a tough guy in a tough sport – rugby league in the 1960s. In those days he would have been described as hard, rough, a no-nonsense, take-no-prisoners sort of player, or perhaps even worse. Whatever, all packs needed characters like Stuart to take and give the flak.

Stuart was signed from the famous Dewsbury amateur club, Shaw Cross. His fee was £750 and he was signed as a loose forward, a position he would rarely fill in his Thrum Hall career. While he is probably best remembered as a hooker, Stuart played in every position in the pack for Halifax and never let the team down. Of his 136 starts, 79 were as hooker, 42 at blind-side prop, 10 in the second-row, 3 at loose forward and 2 at open-side prop. He was six feet tall and weighed thirteen stones when he began at Halifax, but was closer to fifteen stones by the time he left.

Wakefield-born Stuart was twenty when he made his first-team debut in 1962 at hooker in a 16-14 victory over Oldham. Jack Scroby and Frank Fox were his props that afternoon. There was little chance of him displacing John Shaw, however, who had just toured as a Lion. In 1963/64 Stuart played mostly reserve-team football and was a member of the superb Halifax 'A' team which pulverised Hull 'A' 48-5 in the Yorkshire Senior Competition Championship final. However, he also had half-a-dozen run-outs with the first team, including Halifax's 25-12 victory over Wakefield Trinity in the semi-final of the Eastern Division Championship. He also

scored his first try in a 31-13 home victory over Leeds.

The 1964/65 season saw him appear in 19 first-team fixtures as Shaw faded out of the picture, only to be replaced by Dave Harrison. Stuart was hooker in Championship play-off victories over Leeds, Featherstone Rovers and Castleford but was superseded by Harrison for the Championship final, when St Helens were defeated. He had, however, done more than enough to earn his winners' medal.

It was a similar story in 1965/66 when he figured in sensational play-off triumphs at Bradford and Swinton, only for Harrison to be preferred for the semi-final against Wigan and a repeat final against Saints.

As Halifax fell away in the years after 1966, Stuart became one of the mainstays of the side, being increasingly used at prop, as hookers like Barry Anderson and Ian Foye were brought in. Never a great try-scorer, he bagged the only pair of his career, from hooker, in a 13-7 Yorkshire Cup win at Doncaster in 1968. It was a great compliment to Stuart's attitude and loyalty that Halifax appointed him as captain for 1969/70, which turned out to be his last season.

**Previous club:** Wakefield Trinity

**Halifax debut:** 20 August 1978 v. Batley
    Yorkshire Cup

**Final Halifax appearance:** 29 April 1984
    v. Rochdale Hornets

**Appearances:** 184 + 5 subs

**Tries:** 44    **Goals:** 4 drop goals    **Points:** 143

**Transferred to:** Mansfield Marksman

Terry Langton was one of those instantly recognisable characters that fans loved. Bearded, sleeves rolled up, stockings often at half mast – he simply looked belligerent. There was not all that much of him – 5' 7" and eleven stones – but his attitude yelled, 'I don't care if everyone else has given up. I'm still going to give them hell. They won't grind me down.' That was Terry – the indestructible man, the iron man, the bloke who never gave up. He was a real handful in attack and defence. Among his 44 tries for Halifax were plenty in which he simply ignored tacklers to run twenty, thirty or forty yards for spectacular touchdowns. His tackling was deadly sure, relentless and more consistent with a man of much bigger proportions.

Terry was born in Leeds and played amateur rugby league for Stanningley but signed professional forms for Wakefield Trinity. He was not a regular at Belle Vue and when Trinity signed England RU scrum-half Mike Lampkowski, it was clear that Terry was surplus to requirements. He proved one of Maurice Bamford's earliest and most inspired signings for Halifax, at a bargain £1,000.

With half-back partner Mick Blacker he galvanised Halifax from a side capable of losing to amateurs Cawoods into a team which could give anyone a hard time. In his first season, 1978/79, Halifax reached the semi-final of the Yorkshire Cup. The following year Terry was crucial in Halifax's surge to the Yorkshire Cup final, to the semi-finals of the Challenge Cup and to promotion to Division One. During the 1979/80 season he played in 35 of Halifax's 36 fixtures and had his most prolific try-scoring campaign with 12. His outstanding form earned him the Halifax Player of the Year award, which he retained in 1980/81, when he scored 10 tries in 32 matches. He was runner-up for the award in 1981/82 and 1982/83 – an unprecedented record at the club.

In 1981/82 Terry was appointed captain but gave up the role after a disagreement with the Halifax management, Tony Garforth taking over. However, Terry was restored to the captaincy for 1982/83 and 1983/84, leading, as always, from the front. Promotion was won in 1981/82 and 1983/84. Towards the close of the 1982/83 season Terry took over at loose forward, with Steve Bond moving into the second-row, and was just as effective as he had been at scrum-half. He actually scored his only hat-trick for Halifax from loose forward in a 43-6 home win against Doncaster, adding a drop goal for good measure.

Halifax followers were deeply disappointed when Terry transferred to Mansfield for a fee of £1,750 before the start of 1984/85, following his old mates Mick Blacker and Ken Loxton to the Midlands.

# Ken Loxton

Scrum-half, loose forward, 1978-1982

**Previous club:** Keighley

**Halifax debut:** 27 March 1978 v. Swinton

**Final Halifax appearance:** 7 May 1982
    v. Doncaster

**Appearances:** 87 + 19 subs

**Tries:** 2  **Goals:** 0  **Points:** 6

**Transferred to:** Bramley

**Honours:** Great Britain

Ken Loxton was one of Maurice Bamford's first signings in the post-Cawoods renaissance at Thrum Hall in 1978, and one of the most influential. Ken cost Halifax £1,000. On the one hand, they were buying a lot of experience, for Ken had thirteen years of first-class rugby league behind him – eight at Huddersfield and five at Keighley. On the other hand he was already thirty years old and, even in his younger days, he had never been particularly quick, which was unusual for a top-class scrum-half.

There was, however, no doubt that Ken was a fine scrum-half. He had reached Test status in 1971, replacing the great Alex Murphy for the third test against New Zealand at Leeds, Great Britain already having lost the series. With Halifax loose forward Tony Halmshaw also making his only Test appearance, Ken helped galvanise Britain to a face-saving 12-3 victory.

With Halifax his great virtues shone brightly. He was a wonderful organiser and general, his speed of thought compensating for a lack of pace, and he was a master at the play-the-ball, giving out judicious passes or making the half-opening upon which others thrived. His bravery was unquestioned and his tackling was a model for any aspiring young player – clean, clinical and frequent.

Try-scoring was not Ken's concern. In a career stretching over eighteen years and more than 450 games, he scored a mere 24 tries and 3 goals. His tally for Halifax was 2. His first, in his fifth appearance, came in a glorious 20-8 Yorkshire Cup victory over Castleford, when he dropped on a ricocheted kick. His second, in his twenty-sixth game, came off a reverse pass from Terry Langton at Batley. His next 80 games were try-less. Not that it mattered in view of the shoals he engineered for teammates.

Ken was at the heart of most of the good times at Halifax between 1978 and 1982 but had the misfortune to miss the Yorkshire Cup final in 1979, missing the first three months of the season after dislocating his collarbone in a friendly at Keighley. He was, however, a key figure in Halifax's drive to the Challenge Cup semi-final in 1980 and to promotion to the First Division.

Most of Ken's games at Halifax were played at loose forward, despite his lack of size, and his combinations with half-backs Terry Langton and Mick Blacker were a delight. Towards the end of his stay at Halifax he even moved into the second row to accommodate Steve Bond at loose forward. For his last two years at Thrum Hall he was assistant to player-coach Blacker. The pair resigned in 1982 and Ken moved to Bramley, playing 31 games for them before a serious back injury sustained at Cardiff on 26 April 1983 brought his distinguished career to an unfortunate end.

# Tommy Lynch
Right-centre, 1952-1956

**Previous club:** Christchurch Marist RU

**Halifax debut:** 1 January 1952 v. Rochdale Hornets

**Final Halifax appearance:** 12 May 1956 v. Hull Championship final

**Appearances:** 188

**Tries:** 111  **Goals:** 9  **Points:** 351

**Transferred to:** Retired

**Honours:** Other Nationalities, Rugby League XIII

Tommy Lynch toured Australia with the 1951 All Blacks, playing in ten matches (8 tries, 1 drop goal). He played in three victorious Tests for New Zealand at second five-eighth, emulating his father, who had played four tests against Australia (1913 and 1914). It was a sensation when Halifax signed Tommy on a five-year £5,000 contract late in 1951, especially when it is remembered that £5,000 was the current world record transfer fee.

Halifax got their money's worth as Tommy proved a centre of classic style in one of Halifax's most popular teams. Of good physique at 5' 10" and over thirteen stones, Tommy was quick, penetrative, durable and very sound defensively, with a nice line in ball-stealing. He is, however, most fondly remembered for his telepathic and baffling combination with Welsh winger Arthur Daniels. The two were almost inseparable on Halifax's right flank for five years, delighting spectators with their reverse passes and dummy movements, which left opponents wondering who had the ball.

Tommy scored on his debut against Rochdale Hornets. It was the first of over a century of tries. By the time he retired he had scored more tries than any Halifax centre before him. In 1952/53 he topped the club try-scorers with 26 in 44 games, earned a Yorkshire League Championship winners' medal and was a try-scorer in Halifax's Championship final defeat by St Helens.

In 1953/54 there was another Yorkshire League medal for him and he appeared in all of Halifax's games against Warrington in the Challenge Cup and Championship finals. His disallowed try in the Odsal Replay was one of the most contentious decisions in any match played by Halifax. Of Irish origin, Tommy must have derived some satisfaction in scoring three tries against the Wire in Belfast and Dublin in exhibition games in May 1954.

The 1954/55 season saw him ever-present in Halifax's 44 fixtures, when he scored a club record 33 tries for a centre, which remained unbroken until Greg Austin beat it in 1990/91. Included were four hat-tricks against Featherstone Rovers (home), Hull KR (home) and Keighley (home and away).

Tommy's last season, 1955/56, yielded him 25 tries in 45 appearances and his form was as dazzling as ever. He scored the winning try against his compatriots, when Halifax downed the New Zealanders 18-17, and, uniquely, played and scored for the New Zealanders as a guest in a benefit match at Castleford. The Halifax three-quarter line ran in 139 tries during the season with Tommy's partner Daniels setting up a post-war club record of 34 tries. Tommy earned a second consecutive Yorkshire Cup-winners' medal against Hull and a third Yorkshire League medal and appeared in Halifax's defeats in the Challenge Cup and Championship finals, his last games for the club.

# Alan Marchant
Scrum-half, 1959-1964

**Previous club:** Featherstone Rovers

**Halifax debut:** 28 November 1959 v. Wigan

**Final Halifax appearance:** 22 August 1964
   v. Batley

**Appearances:** 151 + 1 sub

**Tries:** 23   **Goals:** 0   **Points:** 69

**Transferred to:** Hunslet

If anyone ever saw a better tackler than Alan Marchant, that person was a most fortunate individual. Alan, all 5' 7" or so and eleven stones of him, could bring down the biggest forwards with unerring classical round-the-legs finality. He would then pat his victim on the head or shoulders like a benign grandfather, as if to say, who's next then? No one ever seemed to get hurt or angry in one of Alan's tackles. They were just too clinical. As a defensive half-back he knew no peers. As a tactical kicker and a strategist, he was also top-notch and he ultimately became a very good captain.

Born in Cutsyke, Castleford, and a miner, he was the younger brother of Jack Marchant, a loose forward who also played at Halifax. Alan graduated from Featherstone Rovers Under-18s to the first team in 1956. In three years at Post Office Road he played 47 first-team games, including Challenge Cup semi-finals in 1958 and 1959, but he was always in the shadow of Don Fox. It was a good move for him when Rovers and Halifax agreed to exchange him for England loose forward Colin Clifft.

Halifax were going through a rebuilding period when Alan arrived at Thrum Hall and Alan had a particularly tough task following in the footsteps of Stan Kielty. In his first few years at Halifax he had a variety of stand-off partners, including Ken Dean, Keith Williams, Keith Fazackerley and Ernie Critchley. In those years there was little success, save for a run to the Challenge Cup semi-final in 1961 against Wigan, when Alan again met with disappointment.

By 1962, he had forged a potent partnership with Barry Robinson and later worked well with Alan Kellett. He was made captain for the 1962/63 season, when Halifax retained their First Division status and qualified for the semi-finals of the Eastern Division Championship and the Yorkshire Cup. The following season, under his leadership, Halifax became a trophy-winning team. The Yorkshire Cup was won, for the last time, when Featherstone were beaten 10-0 at Wakefield, and Alan played one of his greatest games when leading 'Fax to a 20-12 victory over Castleford in the final of the Eastern Division Championship at Fartown.

Elected captain again in 1964/65, matters turned sour when Halifax decided to part with him and promote the young Paul Daley, an altogether different type of scrum-half. Although captain, Alan made only one appearance before being sold to Hunslet for £3,500. That last appearance, against Batley, was historic, however, for he became the first official substitute to appear for the club.

Alan finally, deservedly, got to play at Wembley with Hunslet, figuring in the classic encounter with Wigan in 1965. His playing career was curtailed by a back injury in 1966.

# John Martin

Second-row forward, 1967-1980

**Previous club:** Siddal ARL

**Halifax debut:** 22 August 1967
    *v. Huddersfield*

**Final Halifax appearance:** 14 September
    1980 *v. Workington Town*

**Appearances:** 241 + 21 subs

**Tries:** 20   **Goals:** 8   **Points:** 76

**Transferred to:** Keighley

Local boy made good. John Martin certainly qualifies for that epithet. John was born in Halifax, attended Ovenden Secondary School and played junior rugby league with Siddal. He signed for Halifax for £500 as a nineteen-year-old in 1967 and gave thirteen years exemplary service to the club, through good times but more often through lean times.

Most of John's games were played in the second row but he also played creditably at prop 24 times and at loose forward 32 times. He was one of those players who was totally reliable, a magnificent tackler, who also put in his share of the hard drives. Try-scoring was not his concern, stopping them was. For a forward who played in so many games, John's disciplinary record was almost unblemished – just one dismissal at Wakefield in 1971.

John actually played for the first team before he played for the reserves, making his debut as a half-time substitute for Jack Scroby. However, it was three years before he made his full first-team debut, partnering Terry Fogerty in a 12-22 loss at Castleford on 27 August 1970. In 1968/69 he played loose forward in all 22 games for Halifax Reserves and won the 'A' team Player of the Year award.

Fully established in the first team from 1970/71, John twice won the Halifax Player of the Year award (1974/75 and 1977/78). In 1977 he won the prestigious James Harrison Trophy for the fairest and most loyal player in Yorkshire, presented by the Yorkshire Federation of Supporters Clubs, becoming the fourth Thrum Haller to be so honoured.

The highlights of his career were Halifax's lifting of the John Player Trophy in 1971/72, a season in which he played 42 matches, and the winning of promotion in 1973/74, although he missed the second half of the latter campaign after suffering cartilage trouble in a Boxing Day derby against Huddersfield. The last half of John's career at Thrum Hall saw Halifax in the doldrums but John continued to put in his usual wholehearted efforts in a losing cause. In the disastrous season of 1977/78, when Halifax famously lost to Cawoods, John played in 28 games, more than any other player.

His value to the club and the esteem in which he was held by the fans was reflected in his testimonial, which realised a club record £2,900 in 1978, an extraordinary amount given the dark days the club was experiencing.

John's last couple of years at Halifax were injury-ridden and he made his last appearance as an open-side prop, his first in that position. He rounded off his professional career with a couple of years at Keighley before joining Sowerby Spartans as player-coach in 1984/85. He also returned to Thrum Hall for a spell in later years as coach to the Colts team.

# Seamus McCallion

Hooker, 1984-1991

**Previous club:** Moldgreen ARL

**Halifax debut:** 26 February 1984 v. Carlisle

**Final Halifax appearance:** 1 December 1991
v. Hull

**Appearances:** 195 + 5 subs

**Tries:** 30   **Goals:** 4 drop goals   **Points:** 124

**Transferred to:** Leeds

**Honours:** RL Chairman's XIII, Yorkshire,
Ireland

Seamus McCallion was arguably Halifax's last real hooker. He played in the dying years of contested scrummaging, an activity which effectively ceased by 1990. He retained the old-fashioned skills of a ball-winner and dummy-half but added to them the athleticism required in the modern era. Weighing twelve and a half stones and standing 5' 8", Seamus was a busy, sharp player round the rucks, who could score burrowing tries from close in, while still maintaining the ability and stamina to tackle all over the field. Unusually for a hooker, he was never dismissed from the field.

A BARLA Great Britain Under-19s tourist to New Zealand in 1983, along with another future Halifax forward Gary Divorty, Seamus had already played four trial games for the newly formed Kent Invicta several months before signing for Halifax on 1 March 1984. It was a couple of years before he displaced Nigel Whitehouse, a hooker of the old school – brilliant in the scrums and a worker – and Test man John Dalgreen, who made a brief return to Thrum Hall.

Seamus had become the first Halifax hooker to score a four-point try when he went over at York on 15 April 1984, and he dropped the first of four drop goals for the club at Bradford almost exactly a year later. Oddly, none of his drop goals were at Thrum Hall.

In 1985/86 Halifax won the Championship and, along with Paul Dixon and Gary Stephens, Seamus played in all 37 of Halifax's fixtures during the season, including the Premiership final against Warrington. The Halifax front row of Geoff Robinson, Seamus and Cavill Heugh was a rare handful for opposing teams. Nine tries was a good return for a hooker and Seamus scored two tries in a game on three occasions.

The following season saw Seamus score probably the most memorable try of his life, when he scrambled over from a play-the-ball in the thirty-third minute of the 1987 Challenge Cup final against St Helens, stretching Halifax's lead to 12-2. He returned to Wembley in 1988 but had to settle for a runners-up medal against Wigan. Season 1987/88 had brought him into the limelight with selection for Yorkshire against Papua New Guinea and for a RL Chairman's XIII which defeated Auckland 12-6, both games being played at Leeds.

Halifax were relegated in 1988/89 but bounced back to Division One in 1990/91. Injury kept him out for much of the season and out of the Second Division Premiership final against Salford and the remaining couple of years he spent at Thrum Hall were also blighted with injuries. In 1995, over three years after he had played his 200th and last game for Halifax, Belfast-born Seamus represented Ireland against Cook Islands in the Emerging Nations final at Bury and in 1996, while on Bramley's books, played in Ireland's first full international match against Scotland.

# Keith Neller
Prop, 1984-1988

**Previous club:** Valleys, Brisbane

**Halifax debut:** 14 October 1984 v. Leigh

**Final Halifax appearance:** 30 April 1988
v. Wigan  Challenge Cup final

**Appearances:** 100 + 2 subs

**Tries:** 15   **Goals:** 0   **Points:** 60

**Transferred to:** Gold Coast Giants

Halifax relied heavily on the power and expertise of four Australian props in the halcyon trophy-winning period of the mid-1980s. Geoff Robinson, Cavill Heugh and Martin Bella were all towering performers in their single seasons at Thrum Hall and remain firmly embedded in the memories of Halifax fans of that time. In their own ways they were all more spectacular players than Keith Neller but none gave better service to the club than the man who was nicknamed 'Cow'.

Keith arrived in 1984 as a twenty-two-year-old with the first wave of Australians imported to Thrum Hall by David Brook. He played for Brisbane Valleys, as did fellow imports Bob Arnold and Scott Nicholls. Keith was a try-scorer on his debut, a 23-16 home win against Leigh, when there were seven Aussies in the team, including fellow debutants Michael Hagan, Paul Langmack and Bob Arnold. Keith did not miss a game after his debut, making 32 appearances and scoring 8 tries in 1984/85.

Standing 6' 1" and weighing over fifteen stones, the fair-haired Queenslander never gave opponents any respite. He was a hard and frequent tackler and a damaging runner, who knew when to let the ball go and rarely went backwards. He was one of those forwards who was going just as strongly at the final whistle as he was when the game started. Of his 100 starts, 49 were as open-side prop, 24 at blind-side and 24 in the second row, while his pace brought him 3 appearances at centre in 1985.

In his first season Halifax got to the semi-finals of the John Player Trophy but because of quota restrictions Keith had to miss the Championship-winning 1985/86 season, returning to play for Valleys. He was back for the 1986/87 campaign, however, which included an appearance against the Kangaroos. His contribution to Halifax's winning of the Challenge Cup was enormous. He played in all the rounds and won the Man of the Match award for his performance in the semi-final defeat of Widnes at Leeds.

The following season Keith and Halifax were back at Wembley. In the first round Keith scored a try in a 60-4 rout of Heworth at York and another in a 30-6 home defeat of Rochdale Hornets in the second round. His greatest contribution to the cause, however, came in the nail-biting semi-final replay against Hull at Elland Road. It was his crucial surging run which provided Tony Anderson with the only try of the tie and gave Halifax a 4-3 victory. The final against Wigan was Keith's last game for Halifax.

He returned to Australia, played four years for Gold Coast in the NSW Premiership and then helped Bilambil Jets to win the Gold Coast Group 18 title in 1993 before finishing with Nerang in 1994, where the player-coach was his 1988 Wembley colleague Bob Grogan.

# Mick O'Byrne
Right-winger, 1979-1985

**Previous club:** Cleckheaton RU

**Halifax debut:** 4 September 1979 v. Hull
BBC2 Floodlit Trophy

**Final Halifax appearance:** 24 February 1985
v. Hull Challenge Cup

**Appearances:** 165

**Tries:** 40 **Goals:** 0 **Points:** 140

**Transferred to:** Mansfield Marksman

Mick O'Byrne made his first appearance at Thrum Hall as a trialist in the 'A' team, announcing his potential with a superb half-the-length-of-the-field try, in which he beat three defenders in an 11-7 victory at Huddersfield on 24 August 1979. He was still a trialist a fortnight later when he made his first-team debut at The Boulevard, where First Division Hull beat Second Division Halifax 8-1 in a preliminary round of the Floodlit Trophy. Five days later he scored his first try in a brilliant 33-2 victory at Whitehaven. It was not until 26 September that Halifax finally signed him.

Mick gave six years good and faithful service to Halifax, being seldom out of the first team and playing 165 games on the wing, all but seven on the right. Graham Garrod was his centre for the first couple of seasons before Malcolm Agar took over the job. Mick was a safe rather than spectacular winger but he was nippy and scored some notable tries when they were needed. Defensively there were no complaints about his work.

In his debut season Halifax reached the final of the Yorkshire Cup but he was 'cup-tied' and unable to play in any of the rounds. Derek Howard, Halifax's right-winger, was badly hurt in the final and Mick took his place for the rest of the season. The campaign was extremely successful as Halifax finished second in the league to gain promotion, while they went out of the Challenge Cup to Hull KR at Headingley in the semi-final. Mick's personal highlight came in the 17-13 first-round victory at Featherstone Rovers, when

he crashed over at the flag for the try which won the tie.

Halifax were unfortunate to suffer relegation in 1980/81, Mick scoring 5 tries in 27 appearances. He did, however, score the team's only hat-trick of the season in a 27-6 home win over Barrow on 21 December 1980. The 1981/82 season brought another promotion with Mick contributing 10 tries in 28 games, only for the following season to see relegation again. Mick made his 100th appearance in a surprise 10-2 victory at Bradford on Boxing Day 1982 but missed the last fourteen games with an internal injury sustained at Warrington.

In 1983/84 he was ever-present in the club's 37 matches and was joint leading try-scorer with Keith Waites, his seventeen touchdowns being the best tally of his career. Halifax won promotion again, Mick rounding off the season with a hat-trick in a 50-9 rout of Rochdale Hornets in the last match.

His final season, 1984/85, was marked by an appearance in the semi-final of the Players Trophy against Hull KR at Leeds. The previous week he scored his last try for the club in a 26-8 Boxing Day drubbing of Bradford Northern at Thrum Hall.

# Garfield Owen
Full-back, 1956-1961

**Previous club:** Newport RU

**Halifax debut:** 1 November 1956 v. Albi

**Final Halifax appearance:** 21 August 1961
   v. Bramley

**Appearances:** 166

**Tries:** 4   **Goals:** 535   **Points:** 1,082

**Transferred to:** Keighley

**Honours:** Welsh XIII, Rugby League XIII

Halifax have had some genuinely great full-backs and one of them was Garfield Owen, who signed for Halifax on 17 October 1956, live on BBC's *Sportsview*, probably a unique occurrence. He was the current Wales RU full-back and the signing was a massive news story. As far as Halifax fans were concerned he fulfilled all expectations.

Born in Llanharan, Garfield was a fine all-round sportsman. He was a fast bowler for Welsh Secondary Schools, schools discus champion of Wales, senior Welsh javelin champion and a fine golfer.

Garfield was a classic full-back. His kicking could hardly have been bettered. He could land goals from almost anywhere in the old-fashioned toe-end style and he was a model of consistency. His punting was prodigious and he was capable of dropping long-distance goals. His fielding of the ball was masterful and his tackling impeccable.

His 'A' team debut saw 3,000 turn up at Thrum Hall to see him boot eight goals against Bradford Northern 'A'. His first-team debut, again uniquely, was a European Championship game in Albi, where he kicked a couple of goals in a 19-11 victory. A month later he landed three goals in Halifax's 6-3

beating of the Australians. At the end of 1956/57 he was selected as reserve for Great Britain's World Cup squad and had amassed 91 goals in 31 matches.

In 1957/58, suffering a rare loss of form, he played in only 20 games but kicked 62 goals. He did, however, earn a Yorkshire League winners' medal, the only trophy Halifax won in his time with them. He also represented a Rugby League XIII against France at Leeds kicking five goals in a 19-8 win. In 1958/59 he was made Halifax captain and landed 102 goals in 28 appearances, adding another goal when he played for a Welsh XIII against France at Toulouse.

In 1959/60 Garfield appeared in all 44 of Halifax's fixtures, scoring 145 goals and 2 tries and failing to score only once. The following season he played in 41 of the club's 42 matches (130 goals, 1 try), failing to score just twice. He kicked three goals against the 1960 New Zealand World Cup team, who beat Halifax 18-12, and played a huge part in Halifax reaching the 1961 Challenge Cup semi-final. He was rewarded by being elected Halifax's Player of the Year for 1960/61, the first time the award was made. He was also awarded the James Harrison Trophy as Yorkshire's best and fairest player.

Much to the chagrin of his admirers Garfield was transferred to Keighley in January 1962, becoming captain-coach and breaking many club records in his four-season stint with the Lawkholme Laners, for whom he amassed 702 points (348 goals, 2 tries).

# Geoff Palmer
Left-centre, 1955-1961

**Previous club:** Rosslyn Park RU

**Halifax debut:** 22 August 1955 v. Warrington

**Final Halifax appearance:** 26 April 1961
   v. Oldham

**Appearances:** 208

**Tries:** 99   **Goals:** 0   **Points:** 297

**Transferred to:** Retired

**Honours:** Cumberland, Tour Trialist (1958)

There have been few more impressive sights at Thrum Hall than Geoff Palmer's devastating bursts through opposing three-quarter lines. A giant of a man, at around 6' 2" and well over fifteen stones, his thundering running had a degree of imperiousness which made him a delight to watch. He was fast too but outside him he had Johnny Freeman, who was even faster. The two were as dangerous a centre-wing partnership as is possible. Over the last four decades only the Austin-Preston partnership has come near to their standard.

A Cumbrian, born in Maryport, Geoff played junior rugby league with Glasson Rangers but made his name in rugby union. He played Army rugby union and made an appearance for Newport but mainly played for Rosslyn Park. In 1955 he played for Middlesex against Lancashire at Twickenham in the County Championship final.

Halifax signed Geoff on 21 May 1955 for a reported fee of £2,000. He was a natural from the start, invariably figuring at left-centre. Only 9 of his 208 games were in anything other than the number four jersey – 7 at right-centre and 2 at right-wing. Halifax almost won everything in his first season, taking the Yorkshire League and Yorkshire Cup and losing in the finals of the Challenge Cup and the Championship. Geoff played in the Yorkshire Cup final against Hull at Headingley after only 12 senior matches. His appearance at Wembley in a 2-13 loss against St Helens was his thirty-ninth senior game. A week later he scored one of Halifax's three

tries against Hull at Maine Road, only for Hull to beat the Thrum Hallers 10-9.

Geoff rattled up 27 tries in 40 games in his debut season, scoring a hat-trick at Huddersfield and four tries in a 68-0 thrashing of Hull KR. In 1956/57 his tally was reduced to 17 in 30 games, including another four-try haul against Whitehaven, but he helped Freeman to a club record 48. A third four-try effort came at Batley in 1957/58, when he captained Halifax, one of the youngest men to do so. He was very unfortunate to miss selection for the 1958 Lions tour after skippering The Greens against The Whites in a tour trial at Swinton. Halifax took the Yorkshire League Championship under his leadership that season.

Geoff played a further three seasons for Halifax, who were, unfortunately, a declining force. The nearest he got to further domestic honours was the semi-final of the Challenge Cup in 1961 against Wigan. After that he only played three more games for 'Fax, giving up the game to pursue his career at the early age of twenty-six. By the time he retired he had claimed 99 tries for Halifax, with three more against Huddersfield in Charity Cup matches taking him past the century.

# Les Pearce
Second-row forward, 1949-1959

**Previous club:** Swansea RU

**Halifax debut:** 23 August 1949 v. Batley

**Final Halifax appearance:** 31 January 1959
    v. Batley

**Appearances:** 120

**Tries:** 16   **Goals:** 0   **Points:** 48

**Transferred to:** Dewsbury

Although he played for Halifax for almost ten years, Les Pearce never really commanded a settled place in the Thrum Hall pack. Even so, he is one of the best remembered forwards of the 1950s when Halifax's pack intimidated and outmuscled the very best the league had to offer. Apart from eight games at blind-side prop in his last two seasons, Les was exclusively a second-rower. Being in contention with such men as Les White, Harold Palin, Harry Greenwood and Albert Fearnley in his early years, and with Fearnley, Derrick Schofield and John Henderson later on, meant it was always a struggle to assure that first-team place.

Nonetheless, Les stuck to his guns and played in some big games for the blue and whites. There were few more combative forwards than Les, who was not given to going backwards. At 6' 1" and 14st 7lbs, this dark-haired, craggy, no-frills Welshman possessed the size, belligerence and persistence required for the hard slog of forward work demanded by coach Dolly Dawson.

Born in Skewen, South Wales, Les made a big reputation with Swansea and played for Glamorgan County before Halifax paid him £500 to turn professional. He scored a try on his debut, playing alongside the giant South African Jack Pansegrouw, in a 27-8 victory over Batley. It was not until 1954/55 that he really began to appear regularly, although he had played against the 1952 Australians, was in the Halifax team which met Warrington in Dublin in May 1954 and earned a Yorkshire League winners' medal in 1953/54. In 1954/55 he was a try-scorer in Halifax's 22-14 victory over Hull in the Yorkshire Cup final and played in the 7-0 replayed final victory over Hull in 1955/56. Season 1955/56 also brought him a second Yorkshire League winners' medal and an appearance at Wembley, when St Helens overcame Halifax 13-2.

In 1955 he was in the Halifax side which beat the New Zealanders 18-17 and in 1956 was a member of the team which defeated the Australians 6-3, Halifax's last victory over the Kangaroos. He collected a third Yorkshire League winners' medal in 1957/58.

A free transfer took him to Dewsbury, where he played a couple of seasons alongside old Halifax colleagues John Thorley, Derrick Schofield and Jack Marchant, as well as future 'Fax coach Maurice Bamford. Les later entered coaching and led Halifax to their John Player Trophy success in 1971/72 and had a second stint as coach at Thrum Hall between 1974 and 1976. He also coached at Dewsbury, Leigh (taking them to Floodlit Trophy victory in 1972/73) and Bramley. In 1975 he was appointed coach to Wales for the World Championship, during the course of which he guided his team to an historic victory over England at Brisbane, effectively depriving England of the title.

# John Pendlebury
Loose forward, 1986-1988

**Previous club:** Salford

**Halifax debut:** 7 December 1986
*v.* Warrington  Players Trophy

**Final Halifax appearance:** 18 December 1988
*v.* St Helens

**Appearances:** 75

**Tries:** 11    **Goals:** 15 + 1 drop goal

**Points:** 75

**Transferred to:** Bradford Northern

**Honours:** Lancashire.

John Pendlebury only played for Halifax for two years and had a similar length of service as a first team coach a decade later. Yet he will always be among the first recalled by fans who had the pleasure of watching him, if only for being the main agent of Halifax's drama-filled winning of the Challenge Cup in 1987.

John had already packed much into a seven-year professional career before arriving at Thrum Hall. As an amateur John had made a big name with Leigh Miners Welfare, winning the County Championship (Under-18s) with Lancashire and playing for Great Britain Youth against France in 1978/79. His senior career began at Wigan, where he demonstrated his versatility by figuring at loose forward, hooker and scrum-half. In his time at Central Park he helped Wigan to win promotion in 1980/81 and to lift the Regal Trophy in 1983. He also played in Lancashire Cup finals in 1980 and 1984 although Wigan lost both, and at Wembley in 1984, when Widnes beat them 19-6, among his teammates being Brian Juliff, Colin Whitfield, Gary Stephens and Mick Scott. Two years with Salford followed, where promotion was won in his first season and he became captain. Towards the end of his time at Weaste he played successfully in the second row.

Halifax signed John on 30 November 1986 for £23,000, despite competition from Barrow, Leigh and Wakefield Trinity. His debut, at scrum-half to Chris Anderson, was inauspicious as Warrington hammered 'Fax 44-10 in a third-round Players Trophy tie. Matters improved drastically, however, as John settled at loose forward and became one of the key members of the team which won at Wembley. He was a try-scorer in the semi-final victory over Widnes but saved the game of his life for the final against St Helens.

Graham Eadie won the Lance Todd Trophy in 1987, but the contribution of John Pendlebury in Halifax's 19-18 victory became legendary. Who else would have come up with the match-saving punch which dislodged the ball from Mark Elia's grasp, as he went over for the potential winner as the game entered its dying moments? Was it a miracle? No, it was just John doing the necessary. John's one-point drop goal represented the difference between victory and defeat.

John was a phenomenal player for, although six feet tall, he was scrawny and looked an unlikely candidate for the pack. He was, however, brave, tough as old boots, a great tackler, a deft handler, a clever kicker and, crucially, always a move ahead of the rest.

In 1987/88 John played more games for Halifax (36) than anyone else, including hooker in the Charity Shield against Wigan on the Isle of Man. He played in a second consecutive Challenge Cup final in 1988. On the way he landed eight goals against Heworth in the first round – just another of his many attributes.

# Wynford Phillips

Blind-side prop, second-row forward, 1958-1964

**Previous club:** Llanelli RU

**Halifax debut:** 8 April 1958 *v.* Featherstone Rovers

**Final Halifax appearance:** 4 January 1964 *v.* Keighley

**Appearances:** 130

**Tries:** 15  **Goals:** 0  **Points:** 45

**Transferred to:** Retired

Wynford Phillips gave up the prospect of a glittering career in Welsh rugby union to turn professional with Halifax in 1957. His fee of £3,000 was huge for a comparative unknown. He had developed into a centre three-quarter of rare promise with Llanelli, partnering international centre Cyril Davies and forming an explosive midfield triumvirate with the legendary stand-off Carwyn James.

Wynford spent a highly successful debut season (1957/58) in the 'A' team, scoring 19 tries and a goal. He played left-centre to Charlie Renilson in the Yorkshire Senior Competition Challenge Cup final at Hull, which was lost 5-16, and in the YSC Championship final at Thrum Hall, when Halifax gained revenge on Hull with a 22-5 victory. Before the season ended he made his first-team debut in a 25-8 win at Featherstone and four days later, on 12 April 1958, was in the Halifax team which clinched the Yorkshire League Championship by beating Batley 22-7 at Thrum Hall.

A miner, Wynford was big (6' and 14st), powerful and skilful but perhaps lacked the pace for a top rugby league centre. Halifax decided his potential was better fulfilled in the pack and in 1958/59 he made 10 first-team appearances in the second row. By 1959/60 he was established as a first-teamer but there were still doubts about his best position. Within a month (8 September-10 October) he turned out at right-centre, left-centre, blind-side prop, second row and left-winger. For the big matches against the Australians and the Yorkshire Cup-semi-final against Hull he played prop.

In 1960/61 Wynford missed most of the season but was a revelation in the latter part when he propped in all four of Halifax's Challenge Cup-ties, which culminated in defeat by Wigan in the semi-final. He added another position to his repertoire when he played his only game at loose forward against Oldham. He also found time to play for the 'A' team in their unsuccessful Championship final at Wakefield Trinity. The 1961/62 season, when First Division status was attained, saw Halifax elect to use him in the second row, primarily with Fred Turnbull as his partner. Wynford excelled the following season, however, at prop and seemed to be developing into a real star in that position.

His last season at Thrum Hall was eventful. He was playing brilliantly and helped 'Fax reach the Yorkshire Cup final. In the second round, however, a miraculous 12-4 victory at Wakefield saw Wynford and Ken Roberts sent off within the first quarter. He was a tower of strength in the semi-final at Dewsbury, which 'Fax won 10-9, and in the 10-0 final victory over Featherstone at Wakefield, when he played second row alongside Terry Fogerty. On Christmas Day 1963 he was sent off in an 8-3 home win against Huddersfield and was serving a three-match suspension, when he retired home to Wales aged twenty-six.

# Graham Pitchforth
Left-winger, 1968-1978

**Previous club:** Shaw Cross ARL

**Halifax debut:** 17 August 1968 v. Workington Town

**Final Halifax appearance:** 27 March 1978 v. Swinton

**Appearances:** 152 + 6 subs

**Tries:** 47   **Goals:** 0   **Points:** 141

**Transferred to:** Blackpool Borough

Graham Pitchforth spent eleven years (1967-78) at Thrum Hall and had nothing tangible to show for them. Most of that period was like the dark ages for Halifax. When the light did break briefly when the John Player Trophy was won in 1971/72, Graham spent the entire season in the reserves and missed the glory. Few men endure eleven years at a club, particularly when there is little success, but Graham never threw the towel in and was one of Halifax's most loyal and serviceable players.

Wakefield-born Graham arrived at Thrum Hall in August 1967 aged nineteen, having cost Halifax a £500 signing-on fee. He spent his first year in the reserves but broke into the first team the following year making his debut in a fine 17-2 victory at Workington Town. Things went very well initially as Graham scored his first try a week later in a 41-10 home rout of Hull KR. His eleventh appearance in the firsts was his biggest match, a 5-12 loss to Leeds at Thrum Hall in the Yorkshire Cup semi-final.

After 14 games in that debut season, Graham made only one appearance, as a substitute, in the next three seasons. Barring his way to a wing spot were the likes of Peter Goodchild, Mike Kelly, Dave Rayner, Derek Tudball and Tony Hepworth. It was not until 14 March 1973 that Graham scored again for the first team, when he bagged both Halifax tries in a 12-7 home defeat of Bramley.

The 1973/74 season was Graham's most productive. He played in all 35 of Halifax's fixtures and was joint leading try-scorer with Bruce Burton, touching down 21 times.

Halifax won promotion from fourth position. Graham scored hat-tricks in a 53-3 home pasting of Doncaster and at Fartown in an 18-10 victory over Huddersfield. In 1974/75 he extended his unbroken run of appearances to 49 before missing a Floodlit Cup-tie against Hull KR on 26 November, 7 tries in 29 appearances being his contribution in a season which ended in relegation.

Graham, fair-haired, 5' 11" and lightly built at 11st 7lbs, played all but four of his games for Halifax on the left wing, although he did have experience at stand-off with the reserves. He was pretty quick and could be relied on to go bravely for the flag, his tally of 47 tries being creditable for the time in which he played.

His last three seasons at Halifax saw the club drop to its lowest point. Graham was offered the poisoned chalice of the captaincy for 1977/78 and was skipper when Cawoods won at Thrum Hall, after taking over on Peter Astbury's departure. He scored his last two tries for Halifax in an 11-13 loss at Blackpool on 11 December 1977. In that last awful season Graham played 24 games – more than anyone but the equally loyal John Martin.

# Alan Prescott

Winger, loose forward, 1943-1948

**Previous club:** Widnes ARL

**Halifax debut:** 25 September 1943
   v. Wakefield Trinity

**Final Halifax appearance:** 25 December 1948
   v. Huddersfield

**Appearances:** 71

**Tries:** 8   **Goals:** 0   **Points:** 24

**Transferred to:** St Helens

**Honours:** Lancashire, England, Great Britain,
   Empire XIII

From 1940 onwards Widnes shut down for the duration of the Second World War and Halifax were the main beneficiaries. A whole series of established and experienced Widnes players guested for Halifax, helping to make them one of the most powerful teams of the war years. Among them were Tommy Shannon, the great Tommy McCue, Gus Malone, Hughie McDowell, 'Dipper' Jones and Harry Millington. Halifax also obtained a sixteen-year-old Widnesian prodigy in Alan Prescott for the princely sum of £50.

Alan went on to become one of the game's most iconic figures with St Helens and Great Britain and a world-class prop forward. In 1943, however, Alan was a novice winger, who made his first-team debut, aged sixteen years and three months, on the right flank outside the veteran Fred Rule, in a 6-15 defeat at Wakefield Trinity. Perversely he scored his first senior try for Huddersfield on 27 December 1943 at Fartown against Halifax! Halifax had loaned him to Huddersfield, who were a man short. To rub salt into a self-inflicted wound, Halifax lost 8-12.

Ironically, Alan's first try for Halifax was scored at Knowsley Road, the scene of many of his subsequent triumphs, on 19 February 1944, when St Helens were beaten 16-9. In 1944/45 he played in Halifax's two-leg Yorkshire Cup final victory over Hunslet and

in the second leg of their Challenge Cup semi-final loss to Huddersfield. He was not selected for either leg of the Championship final against Bradford Northern, however.

It was not until 27 October 1945 that Alan played first-team rugby as a forward, when he packed down in the second row with Mel Meek in a 20-2 victory at Liverpool Stanley, scoring a try. Two years in the army elapsed before he reappeared against the 1947 New Zealanders as a loose forward, Halifax losing 5-21. He was still packing down last a year later, on 27 November, when Halifax gave the Australians a close encounter before going down 8-10. Alan's final game for Halifax was on Christmas Day 1948, when Huddersfield hammered them 32-3 at Fartown.

Three weeks later he made a try-scoring debut for ambitious St Helens in a 17-5 win at Belle Vue Rangers, the first of over 400 games he would play for Saints. Halifax had received £2,000 for the rampaging, red-haired forward, a large return on their £50 investment. A few months after Alan left he was back at Thrum Hall playing for Lancashire against Yorkshire. He did miss the opportunity to play at Wembley with Halifax in 1949 but made up for that. In 1953 he was in the Saints' front row when they beat Halifax in the Championship final at Maine Road. Three years later he captained Saints to their first ever Challenge Cup, also against Halifax, winning the Lance Todd Trophy as well.

# Mark Preston
Left-winger, 1991-1996

**Previous club:** Wigan

**Halifax debut:** 1 September 1991 v. Featherstone Rovers

**Final Halifax appearance:** 25 February 1996 v. Leeds Challenge Cup

**Appearances:** 131 + 4 subs

**Tries:** 90 **Goals:** 0 **Points:** 360

**Transferred to:** Fylde RU

**Honours:** Lancashire

Mark Preston was certainly the most exciting left-wingman to represent Halifax since the retirement of Johnny Freeman. Small, compact and electric in pace, Preston set the Thrum Hall terraces alight whenever he was afforded any space in which to run. There were few, if any, faster men playing the game in Mark's time (1988-96) and that includes such speedsters as Martin Offiah and Anthony Sullivan. How the international selectors managed to overlook Mark Preston simply beggars belief. Some of his tries were absolutely breathtaking – combinations of sheer pace and baffling evasiveness.

Born in Lytham St Anne's, Mark made his reputation in rugby union with Fylde. His last game before turning professional was for England 'B' against Italy 'B' at Leicester, when among his colleagues were John Bentley and Sheffield scrum-half David Holmes, both of whom later played with Halifax. He signed for Wigan, for whom he ran in 57 tries in 84 appearances. Included were two cracking tries in the 1990 Challenge Cup final, when Warrington were beaten 36-14 at Wembley. He also won a Championship medal that season and was in the Wigan team which beat Halifax in the Regal Trophy final the following season. He twice scored five tries in a game for Wigan and in 1989/90 topped their tries (32) and appearances (41) lists.

Halifax signed Mark for £60,000 in June 1991 and it was soon clear he was well worth

the outlay. He scored on his debut and in his seventh appearance he raced over for four tries in a 76-8 victory over Hull KR. His first season brought him 27 tries in 32 appearances and he had a run of scoring in seven consecutive games. His first two seasons saw him playing outside Greg Austin – he was probably the only man who could keep up with the flying Austin – and he scored 50 tries in 62 matches in that time.

Mark put together a run of 48 consecutive matches for Halifax in that period to confound those who regarded him as too small. When Austin left the club Mark's scoring opportunities diminished and it was a real frustration for the fans, who were denied the thrills he could undoubtedly provide with even a half-decent service. Even so, he managed to add another 40 tries to his tally in much leaner times. In his last full season, 1994/95, he bagged 21 tries in 31 games.

The advent of Super League effectively drove Mark Preston out. He did not want to be a full-time player and Halifax were not flexible enough to accommodate his wishes, resulting eventually in his return to Fylde as a professional rugby union player, after a few games on loan to Widnes. The loss of such a crowd-pleaser and match-winner was one of the club's biggest gaffes of the modern era.

# Gareth Price

Centre, 1949-1951

**Previous club:** Leeds

**Halifax debut:** 5 February 1949 v. Salford

**Final Halifax appearance:** 28 April 1951
v. Swinton

**Appearances:** 87

**Tries:** 22    **Goals:** 1    **Points:** 68

**Transferred to:** Doncaster

**Honours:** Wales, Rugby League XIII, tour trial
(1946)

Some players make an enormous difference to the way a team performs. They are catalysts, galvanising forces, men who make others play. Gareth Morgan Price was one such man.

Halifax certainly needed a saviour in 1949. After being one of the most successful and powerful teams in the game in the immediate pre-war and war years, a steady decline had set in at Halifax, who had finished fourteenth in 1945/46, twentieth in 1946/47 and eighteenth in 1947/48 and got nowhere in the cup competitions. The 1948/49 season was shaping up similarly as Challenge Cup time approached. By February 1949 they had won only seven of their twenty-three league fixtures and were firmly ensconced in the depths. During the season no fewer than forty-three players were used, twenty-two of them debutants. Things were dire.

The Halifax board entered the transfer market and there was considerable turnover of players, but with little improvement. Then they got lucky, or made an inspired choice. Gareth Price was signed from Leeds for a club record fee of £2,750 on 1 February 1949. He was appointed player-coach – a novel idea for the Thrum Hallers. Gareth was already thirty-one but he was a centre of high repute, having won 11 caps for Wales since his two-try debut in an 11-3 win over England at Swansea in the first post-war international on 24 November 1945. He was a native of Llangennech and had played union for Llanelli before joining Leeds for £400 in 1938.

Army service kept him out of the game for almost all the war years. Otherwise he would have won many more caps and may have earned a Lions tour. He did, however, have a tour trial in 1946 when he partnered Halifax's winger Arthur Bassett. He played for Leeds in the 1947 Challenge Cup and was their leading try-scorer in 1945/46 and 1946/47.

Gareth was an astute footballer. He was tall (5' 11") but not heavy (around twelve stones) and creative. He ran elusively, had a disconcerting swerve and side-step, could make openings for others and was a strong defender. Crucially he had pronounced leadership qualities. 'D'Artagnan' wrote of him in *Rugby League Review* in 1951, 'Gareth Price did not wave a magic wand over his men, nor did he make them into a team of world-beaters. But he did make them into a team. He brought steadiness into the back division and his intelligent play both on defence and attack had its effect. He proved an ideal leader, always ready with the word of praise and a pat on the back, and his coolness under pressure had an inspiring influence on the Halifax players.'

Gareth made his debut in a 13-4 home victory over Salford and was partnered by another debutant, Paddy Reid, a former Irish rugby union cap, who had cost £2,500 from Huddersfield. It was to be a short-lived but fruitful pairing. Halifax then beat Hull 10-4 on aggregate in the first round of the Cup, having lost the first leg at Hull 0-4. Thus began a run of amazing, close-fought Cup-ties,

*Gareth Price and Ernest Ward lead out their teams at Wembley in 1949. Price is followed by full-back Dennis Chalkley, who died in November 2003, as this book was in preparation.*

which brought 'Fax back from the dead. Gareth's men had to recover from the death of winger David Craven, whom Gareth partnered in his third game, a 4-4 home draw with Workington Town, on 26 February. David was injured in a tackle and died a few days later. It said much for the character and resolve of Gareth and his players that they overcame the tragedy so well.

Swinton were beaten 5-0 at Thrum Hall in the cup second round and then Oldham were dramatically ousted 7-2 at Watersheddings. The semi-final, before 61,875 at Odsal, produced one of the biggest shocks in the competition's history, when Huddersfield were pipped 11-10 by a fortuitous late try from Stan Kielty. Incredibly Gareth had steered Halifax to Wembley, having only played seven games for the club. It did not matter too much that 'Fax lost 0-12 to Bradford Northern in the final and that Halifax still finished twenty-fifth in the table. He had taken a rag-tag team, containing Maoris, Irishmen, Welshmen, Lancastrians, Yorkshiremen, a Cumbrian, a Northumbrian and a South African, to the Challenge Cup final against all expectations and put Halifax back on the map. That Wembley team, however, never played as a unit again.

Gareth worked his magic the following season, when Halifax rose to fourth and took Wigan to a replay in the Championship semi-final, watched by 28,150 at Thrum Hall. His own performances were as good as ever. He played in 34 matches, mostly at right-centre to fellow countryman Arthur Daniels. By now the nucleus of the great team of the early and mid-1950s had been gathered – Dean and Kielty, at half-back, Daniels, Alvin Ackerley and Les White were all established and Jack Wilkinson and Les Pearce were just coming through, while Peter Todd and Albert Fearnley arrived in 1950/51.

For the 1950/51 season Gareth, a newsagent, gave up the captaincy to Arthur Daniels but proved his value by scoring 14 tries in 38 appearances, turning out in both centre positions, right-wing, full-back and stand-off. He scored all three of Halifax's tries in a 17-0 home win against Keighley. Gareth was honoured with the captaincy of a Welsh XIII which met an Empire XIII at Llanelli on 19 May 1951, as part of the game's contribution to the Festival of Britain.

It could fairly be said that the roots of Halifax's great side of the 1950s were planted and nourished by Gareth Price, who returned briefly to Halifax as coach in October 1958, replacing his own successor, Dolly Dawson.

# Dave Rayner

Winger, 1968-1975

**Previous club:** Batley

**Halifax debut:** 3 February 1968 v. Leigh
    Miners Welfare  Challenge Cup

**Final Halifax appearance:** 14 September
    1975 v. Bramley  BBC2 Floodlit Trophy

**Appearances:** 122 + 1 sub

**Tries:** 44   **Goals:** 0   **Points:** 132

**Transferred to:** Retired

**Honours:** Rugby League XIII

Local boy Dave Rayner arrived at Halifax by circuitous routes, twice. After playing with Ovenden, he signed for Batley, for whom he played 128 games in four seasons. Halifax acquired his services for £2,000 in February 1968, thereby ending a run of 73 consecutive appearances for the Gallant Youths. While a Batley player Dave had represented a Rugby League XIII against a Paris XIII at the Parc des Princes on 5 May 1966.

Dave scored the first of 44 tries for Halifax on his debut, a 24-7 win against Leigh Miners Welfare in a first round Challenge Cup-tie, when Cumbrian second-rower Bill Kirkbride also made his debut. For the next three years Dave became Halifax's regular left-winger. He topped the try-scorers in 1969/70 with 12 tries in 25 appearances. Dave scored some lovely tries for Halifax, being a speedy and elusive runner. His solid 5' 9" and twelve-stone frame took some buffeting in his determined efforts to breach defences but if a try was in the offing Dave would find a way through.

In 1969/70 and 1970/71 Halifax scraped into the Top Sixteen play-offs but never got past the first round. The 1971/72 season saw them fail to qualify for the play-offs but nonetheless have a successful season. Dave played a massive 45 games for 'Fax in 1971/72,

just one fewer than his centre partner Phil Davies, who topped the appearances chart. By this time Dave had switched to the right wing. He led the try-scorers with 17 and played a considerable part in Halifax's winning of the John Player Trophy. Dave claimed tries in the 16-9 first-round win at Warrington and the 36-13 third round victory over Barrow at Thrum Hall. The most significant try of his career, however, came in the semi-final at Headingley. Halifax beat Leeds 15-7 on their own midden and Dave produced a wonderful try, following his own kick, grabbing the ball from under a defender's nose on halfway and side-stepping two more tacklers before racing triumphantly to the posts. His winners' medal from the final victory over Wakefield Trinity at Odsal was well deserved.

Dave played in all the rounds of Halifax's surge to the Challenge Cup semi-final later that season but ended his first spell at the club by emigrating with his family to Australia in May 1972. He became associated with the Wentworthville club in New South Wales and directed several Aussies to Thrum Hall in the following two years. He then returned to England and rejoined Halifax, reappearing in the Charity Cup match against Huddersfield on 16 August 1974, when he was twice cautioned in altercations with Fartown skipper Ken Senior – not an uncommon occurrence in the old-time Charity clashes! His professional career ended with just 3 more first-team appearances for Halifax.

# Derek Reeves

Second-row forward, utility player, 1964-1972

**Previous club:** Bramley Old Boys RU

**Halifax debut:** 17 April 1964 v. Wigan

**Final Halifax appearance:** 1 October 1972 v. Leigh

**Appearances:** 150 + 23 subs

**Tries:** 27   **Goals:** 0   **Points:** 81

**Transferred to:** Keighley

Halifax signed Derek Reeves for £600 in March 1964 from Bramley Old Boys RU Club, from where they had also signed Dave Stockwell and Eddie Gill in recent times. Derek had been a Yorkshire RU trialist but had represented Leeds Schools at rugby league. At the time Halifax thought they were signing a centre/stand-off but Derek made his mark eventually at second row.

He was, however, possibly the most versatile player Halifax ever had, barring Welshman Jack Beames, who played before, during and after the First World War. Derek, at 5' 10" and maybe fourteen stones in his latter days but certainly not his early career, made first-team starts at full-back (2 games), wing (1), centre (4), scrum-half (2), blind-side prop (17), hooker (4), second row (113) and loose forward (7) for Halifax. The only positions he did not fill were stand-off, although he appeared there many times for the reserves, and open-side prop. Often he would play in several positions during matches, covering for any injuries, mishaps, substitutions or tactical considerations. With Derek it really was a case of rolling up his sleeves and getting on with the job. The fans admired his pluck, industry and total reliability.

Within a month of signing he made his debut in a 3-3 draw at Wigan, playing right-centre in a team which contained nine reserves. Duncan Jackson, his winger, scored the equalising try. In 6 'A' team appearances he scored 7 tries, including one in Halifax's 48-5 mauling of Hull 'A' in the final of the Yorkshire Senior Competition Shield.

For the next four years Derek was a mainstay of the 'A' team, displaying his versatility. On Boxing Day 1967 he played in the forwards for the first time at first-team level, forming an unlikely second row partnership with Stuart Kelley in a 10-8 win at Bradford.

By 1968/69 he had established a regular place in the team, playing well above his weight in the pack. Such was his form and popularity he was appointed captain for 1970/71, when he played in all 38 of Halifax's fixtures and registered a personal best haul of 10 tries. From 14 December 1969, when he was a try-scorer in an 18-10 victory at York, he played in 57 consecutive matches.

He retained the captaincy for 1971/72 leading Halifax to the John Player Trophy final but having to be content with a seventy-fourth-minute appearance as substitute in the victory over Wakefield Trinity at Odsal. In 1972/73 Derek was a try-scorer in Halifax's record-breaking 76-8 win at Hunslet in the Yorkshire Cup first round and he played in Halifax's 10-19 Yorkshire Cup semi-final defeat at Dewsbury before moving to Keighley for a reported fee of £700. He played on at Keighley until the close of the 1973/74 season, making 33 appearances (3 tries).

# Charlie Renilson
Loose forward, 1957-1969

**Previous club:** Jed-Forest RU

**Halifax debut:** 12 October 1957 v. Barrow

**Final Halifax appearance:** 26 March 1969
v. Batley

**Appearances:** 299 + 3 subs

**Tries:** 70   **Goals:** 19   **Points:** 248

**Transferred to:** Newtown, Australia

**Honours:** Commonwealth XIII, Great Britain

One of the great heroes and most popular players of the 1960s was Charlie Renilson, one of a very rare species – a Scot who made it to the very top in rugby league. Charlie was a six-foot, 14st 3lbs whirlwind of a player. Fair-haired and athletic, Charlie was a cover defender *par excellence*, with a classic tackling style and, although a sporting and clean player, he was as tough as old boots. On attack he could be devastating, for he was as fast as many three-quarters, had the speed to go through a gap and the strength to go through a man, supported well, and was a consistent try-scorer. He was not a loose forward in the mould of the two who were at Thrum Hall when he arrived there in 1957 – Ken Traill and Colin Clifft, both internationals with great ball skills and tactical brains. His style was much more physical and direct but he would emulate Traill and Clifft in winning international recognition.

Charlie was born in Jedburgh and played for Jed-Forest in the Scottish Borders. In 1957 he followed in the footsteps of his uncle Billy Renilson, who had come south to Halifax as a three-quarter in 1925. Although just a teenager, Charlie received a fee of £1,500. On his debut he kicked two goals in a 15-15 home draw against Willie Horne's Barrow, his first five games yielding him three tries and eleven goals. In his fourth game Charlie equalled the club record for a forward by scoring seven goals (plus a try) in a 62-2 massacre of Dewsbury on 9 November 1957, thus emulating three famous 'Fax forwards, all Internationals, Fred Longstaff, Nat Bentham and Harold Palin.

However, it was to be several years before Charlie became a regular first-teamer. His first season saw him play 10 games as a second-rower but he played on the wing for the 'A' team in the Yorkshire Senior Competition Challenge Cup and Championship finals against Hull 'A', losing the former and winning the latter. He first appeared at loose forward at senior level against Doncaster on 25 October 1958. His ninth and last game of the 1958/59 season was against Wigan in the third round of the Cup, when a record Thrum Hall crowd of 29,153 was recorded.

In 1959/60 he appeared against the Kangaroos as a second-rower but was at loose forward in his first Yorkshire Cup semi-final at Hull. For the next two seasons there was little first team rugby for Charlie, who played a great deal of rugby union in the Army and was posted for long periods to Kenya. He played in the Inter-Services Tournament against the Navy and the RAF at Twickenham in 1961 and in Army Cup finals for the Duke of Wellington's Regiment. He still found time, however, to play for Halifax in the 1961 Challenge Cup semi-final against Wigan and to win the inaugural Halifax 'A' team Player of the Year award in 1961/62.

The 1962/63 season was going splendidly for Charlie and, having played in the semi-finals of the Yorkshire Cup and Eastern Division, he was to have won his first Test cap against France, as a replacement for Derek Turner, when he broke his arm against Hull and missed the last fifteen games.

*Castleford's defence is left in tatters as Charlie Renilson scores a spectacular try.*

Fully recovered for 1963/64, Charlie was a try-scorer in Halifax's Yorkshire Cup final victory over Featherstone and by the end of the season was part of a superb back three with Colin Dixon and Terry Fogerty, which spearheaded Halifax's win over Castleford in the Eastern Division Championship final.

In 1964/65 Charlie topped the forward try-scorers with 12 in 37 appearances and displayed scintillating form as Halifax swept to the Championship, scoring twice against Leeds in the play-offs and a crucial try at Castleford in the semi-final.

At the start of the 1965/66 campaign Charlie played for the Commonwealth against New Zealand at Crystal Palace, along with Ronnie James and Terry Fogerty, and won his first test cap against the Kiwis at Swinton, scoring the only try in a 7-2 victory. At the season's end Charlie played in his second Championship final against St Helens, having been a try-scorer in the semi-final victory at Wigan, but 'Fax were well beaten.

The 1966/67 season saw Charlie again top the forward try-scorers with 11, including the only hat-trick of his career in a 45-14 win at Hunslet. During the first half of the season he moved to second row, allowing John Burnett to play loose forward. The following season

was huge for Charlie. He received a record benefit of £1,650, shared the Player of the Year award with David Jones, bagged another 10 tries for the club, including two from the wing at Keighley, appeared in the third Ashes Test, and played for Great Britain in victories over France at Paris and Bradford. He was arguably the best loose forward in England and richly deserved his selection for the Great Britain World Cup squad, which went Down Under in the summer of 1968. Charlie played in all three matches and in the four subsequent up-country games in Queensland.

Charlie's career at Thrum Hall concluded after the 1968/69 season. Halifax reached the semi-final of the Yorkshire Cup, losing at home to Leeds, when Charlie played at blindside prop. Great Britain still thought he was their best loose forward, however, and he starred in a 34-10 slaying of France at St Helens in his last Test match on 30 November 1968. By coincidence, it was Colin Dixon's test debut.

Charlie joined the Sydney club Newtown in 1969, Halifax receiving £2,000. He played 54 games (6 tries) for them and captain-coached their reserve-grade team to the Premiership in 1970, before playing briefly for Eastern Suburbs.

# Ken Roberts

Open-side prop, second-row forward, 1963-1967

**Previous club:** Swinton

**Halifax debut:** 24 August 1963 v. Featherstone Rovers

**Final Halifax appearance:** 27 January 1967 v. Leeds

**Appearances:** 124 + 3 subs

**Tries:** 6　**Goals:** 0　**Points:** 18

**Transferred to:** Bradford Northern

**Honours:** Lancashire, Great Britain

Ken Roberts' career as a Thrum Haller was relatively short – just three and a half years. His impact, however, was immense. Halifax had the makings of a successful side when he arrived at the club in August 1963 but it was his, and stand-off Alan Kellett's, integration into that team which sparked the glory days of the mid-1960s.

Ken was one of those rare forwards who had the ability to dominate games through sheer physical power and/or sublime ball-handling skills. He sprang from the same mould as Arthur Clues, Malcolm Reilly, Artie Beetson and Lee Crooks – men who could deal in mayhem or magic. At 6' 1" and over sixteen stones when he joined 'Fax, Ken was an intimidating figure on a rugby field, in anyone's language. Expressions such as 'backwards', 'flinch' and 'give in' were not in his lexicon. He was prepared to meet fire with fire, was a damaging defender, a hard and surprisingly quick runner and a force in the tight scrums. On top of all that, he was an inspiring pack leader, who always took the game to the opposition. In short, he was a player to be feared, respected and admired.

In the early 1960s it was still unusual for players to cross the Pennines and Ken was a Lancastrian, who was born in Atherton, played rugby union for Tyldesley and became a rugby league professional with Swinton. He

also cost Halifax a whopping £5,000, or £5,500 according to some reports. Once they realised what an asset he was, Halifax fans were happy to forget about his ancestry and the expense! Ken became an adopted son of Halifax, remaining in the town, returning to the club as coach for a brief spell in 1982 and is currently a respected and popular chairman of the Halifax Past Players Association.

Almost twenty-six years of age when he joined Halifax, Ken had packed a lot of experience into seven years as a Swinton first-teamer. He had played 202 games for the Lions, scoring 30 tries and 19 goals. He had played in three losing Lancashire Cup finals but had gained a Lancashire League winners medal in 1960/61 and had been a key member of the team which won the First Division Championship in 1962/63. He had also been capped by Lancashire.

Ken came to Halifax as a second-rower and played in that position for most of his debut season, usually alongside his fellow Lancastrian Terry Fogerty. Ken's clever, robust play energised the already powerful Halifax pack. The immediate result was a first Yorkshire Cup final for eight years, although he had to sit out the final victory over Featherstone Rovers, having been sent off, along with Wyn Phillips, in Halifax's win at Wakefield Trinity in the second round. By the time Halifax reached their second victorious final of the campaign against Castleford in the Eastern Division Championship, Ken had

*There is no escape for this New Zealander as Ken Roberts and Duncan Jackson combine to halt his progress at Thrum Hall in 1965.*

settled into what became his accustomed position of open-side prop.

In 1964/65 Ken was elected vice-captain but was thrust quickly into the captaincy when Alan Marchant left for Hunslet. He held the reins until January 1965 before relinquishing them to John Burnett. Ken's leadership of a magnificent set of forwards was a colossal factor in Halifax's surge to the Championship final and it was their dominance which allowed Halifax to overcome St Helens 15-7. During that momentous season he made 39 appearances.

Ken was vice-captain again in 1965/66, when Halifax lost 12-35 to St Helens in a repeat Championship final at Swinton. His 36 appearances included the fixture against the New Zealanders, which was lost 12-24, and he also had the novel experience of playing sevens for Halifax at Crystal Palace, as part of the long-forgotten Commonwealth Festival of Sport. His last season, 1966/67, at Thrum Hall saw him take over the captaincy from John Burnett and Halifax almost reached the Yorkshire Cup final, losing to Featherstone in the semi-final. He was, however, transferred to Bradford Northern, in exchange for Stan Fearnley, just before the Challenge Cup transfer deadline in February 1967.

Subsequent transfers took Ken to Rochdale Hornets and Salford and he retired in 1970 having made no fewer than 475 appearances in first-class rugby league.

Ken was a forward of the very highest class and, until Karl Harrison came along a quarter of a century later, he remained Halifax's most capped Test player with 10 appearances for Great Britain. His Test career began in 1963 when Great Britain called him up in the second row for the third Ashes Test at Headingley. The first two Tests had been lost, heavily and embarrassingly, and Ken's debut Test was one of the most brutal of all Ashes clashes, which is saying something. A completely revamped Great Britain side salvaged a 16-5 victory from a torrid game, which saw three players dismissed. Ken was a towering figure throughout, always where the struggle was fiercest and soaking up all the Aussies could throw at him.

Winning tests against the French at Perpignan and Leigh followed in 1964, and by 1965, as a prop, he was vice-captain to Tommy Smales in a victorious home series against New Zealand. In 1966 he toured Australasia with the Lions, figuring in two successful tests against New Zealand. No Halifax player has captained a British Test team but Ken did captain Great Britain XIIIs against Central Queensland, Newcastle, Southern New South Wales, Northern Division and Monaro. He played nineteen games on tour, scoring four tries.

Ken has kept up his British Lions connections and is a committee member of the British Rugby League Lions Association.

# Barry Robinson
Stand-off, 1959-1971

**Previous club:** Shaw Cross ARL

**Halifax debut:** 17 October 1959 v. Hull Kingston Rovers

**Final Halifax appearance:** 11 September 1971 v. Hull Kingston Rovers

**Appearances:** 263 + 14 subs

**Tries:** 73  **Goals:** 1  **Points:** 221

**Transferred to:** Retired

Over a period of twelve years Barry Robinson gave Halifax wonderful service and won the respect of the Thrum Hall fans for his wholehearted effort, willingness to play anywhere and refusal to take umbrage whenever Halifax bought in another stand-off. As a stand-off Barry's greatest virtue was his indefatigable backing up. He was not the quickest or most constructive of stand-offs but he was a fine all-purpose player, alert enough to be a regular try-scorer, a jinker and side-stepper and a fine defender. His handling was excellent – he seemed to have fly-paper hands, which safely gathered in the most awkward of passes. Tousle-haired and broad-faced, he rejoiced in three nicknames – Twinkle Toes, Flat Feet and Tivvy – a singular distinction for any player.

Wakefield-born Barry was a Yorkshire Under-19s stand-off when he signed for Halifax in 1959. Halifax saw him as the successor to Ken Dean, which was a tall order. He played his first few games at scrum-half alongside Dean, his third first-team appearance being against the Kangaroos. Towards the end of the 1960/61 season Barry was the stand-off and had his first experience of a big stage playing against Wigan at Swinton in the Challenge Cup semi-final.

By 1962/63 Barry had a well-established half-back partnership with Alan Marchant as Halifax developed into a side capable of challenging for honours. He scored a personal-best 14 tries that season, including his first hat-trick in a 33-12 rout of Featherstone Rovers, and he played in the semi-finals of the Yorkshire Cup and Eastern Division Championship. In 1963/64 Halifax won both those competitions with Barry playing at stand-off in both finals, despite the introduction of Alan Kellett. He scored a vital try in the 20-12 victory over Castleford in the Eastern Division final at Fartown.

Late in 1964/65 Barry and Paul Daley proved a lethal half-back pairing as Halifax swept to their great Championship final triumph against St Helens at Swinton. Earlier in the campaign Barry had been shuttled between scrum-half and left-centre and had even played on the left wing against Bradford Northern, when he bagged two tries in a 24-3 win. In 1965/66 he was a try-scorer in Halifax's 12-24 loss to the New Zealanders and played in his last major final when Halifax lost to St Helens 12-35 in the Championship final, suffering a cut head.

Halifax declined over the next five years but Barry still played a couple of Yorkshire Cup semi-finals for the blue and whites and appeared against the 1967 Australians. In 1967/68 he played in more games (42) than any player and registered his second and last hat-trick in a 35-12 win over Doncaster. After retiring, Barry played as an amateur, captaining Ossett Trinity.

# Paul Rowley
Number nine, 1994-2000

**Previous club:** Leigh

**Halifax debut:** 13 November 1994
    v. St Helens

**Final Halifax appearance:** 10 September
    2000 v. Salford

**Appearances:** 162 + 8 subs

**Tries:** 40   **Goals:** 1 + 3 drop goals

**Points:** 165

**Transferred to:** Huddersfield

**Honours:** Great Britain Under-21s, Emerging
    England, England

Halifax recruited heavily in the Leigh area in the 1990s and the best of their acquisitions was undoubtedly Paul Rowley. A former Leigh Miners player, Paul had already played over 50 first-team games for Leigh when he signed for Halifax on 8 November 1994 but was still only nineteen. Fellow Leigh forward Simon Baldwin signed around the same time. Paul had already played twice for Great Britain Academy against the Junior Kiwis in 1993 and twice against France in 1994. He went on to star in the 1994 Academy tour of Australia.

In former times Paul would probably have been a tremendous scrum-half but the game of the 1990s dictated that he was best used at number nine. His speed away from the rucks was a big advantage to his team and he supported the ball-carriers well and often. Paul was quite capable of running in tries from halfway, having the eye for an opening and the pace to carry him through it. Some of his tries were quite spectacular and his defence was extremely solid.

Paul scored a try with his first touch of the ball for Halifax at St Helens in a desperately unlucky 14-18 defeat and quickly established himself as a fans' favourite. Oddly enough, however, his six years at Thrum Hall and The Shay were bedevilled by rumours and press reports that he was about to leave the club. He did not leave and always played with spirit

and enthusiasm. By the end of his first season at Halifax Paul had won Great Britain Under-21 selection, along with Baldwin, against the French. In 1996 he won an England cap, being a sixty-first-minute substitute for Johnny Lawless, then a Sheffield player, in a 73-6 massacre of France at Gateshead.

The 1996 season saw him play in 24 fixtures, more than any other Halifax player. The following season he was part of the Halifax team which suffered record defeats down under against Canberra and Brisbane but 1998 saw a great improvement as Halifax finished third in Super League. Paul was an ever-present (27 games) during 1998, having the benefit of being propped by Karl Harrison and Kelvin Skerrett. Paul played in the last first-team game at Thrum Hall against Leeds on 22 March 1998 and went on to play for Emerging England in their 15-12 defeat of Wales at Widnes. Surprisingly, that was his last representative honour. How the Great Britain selectors overlooked him for the 1999 Tri-series in Australia and New Zealand remains a mystery, particularly as Keiron Cunningham was clearly unfit in those games.

In his last season at Halifax, 2000, Paul scored 10 tries – his best return for the club – and kicked his only place goal in his last match. Paul is currently playing for Leigh in National League One.

Scrum-half, stand-off, 1969-1975

**Previous club:** Normanton ARL

**Halifax debut:** 7 August 1969 v. Wakefield Trinity Yorkshire Cup

**Final Halifax appearance:** 28 September 1975 v. New Hunslet Players Trophy

**Appearances:** 142 + 30 subs

**Tries:** 47   **Goals:** 6 + 1 drop goal

**Points:** 154

**Transferred to:** Wakefield Trinity

A scrum-half in the traditional mode, Sammy Sanderson spent six years at Thrum Hall, mostly in lean times, but is well remembered by 'Fax followers of the period. Only 5' 4" tall and 10st 8lb, Sammy was a typical, cheeky, boyish-looking number seven. He was always somewhere near the action, probing, urging, trying whatever came into his head and a thorough nuisance to opposing teams. He was not a great defender, his strengths being more geared to attacking activities, nippiness and a competent kicking game.

Born in Normanton in 1950, Sammy played for the local amateur team and signed for Halifax for £550, making his first-team debut as an eighteen-year-old. Throughout his Thrum Hall career Sammy had to contend with the more experienced Gordon Baker for the scrum-half position, the two being very different in style. The fact that both were usually accommodated in the same team was a testament to Sammy's ability to fill in at stand-off, where he made 38 appearances, and Gordon's capacity to play loose forward. Often one or the other acted as substitute.

When Baker was injured in 1970/71 Sammy got his first extended run as scrum-half to Alan Kellett, and then fitted in for Kellett when Baker returned. The following season saw him strike up a fruitful partnership with the rising stand-off star Bruce Burton.

Even so, it was Baker who got the nod in Halifax's team for the John Player Trophy final against Wakefield Trinity at Odsal, Sammy coming on late as a substitute in a 22-11 victory. He was also used off the bench in Halifax's loss to Leeds at Odsal in the Challenge Cup semi-final later in the season. Sammy played in 43 games in 1971/72.

In 1972/73 he appeared in 36 games, 19 at stand-off, including a Yorkshire Cup semi-final defeat at Dewsbury. He finished as leading try-scorer with 18, among which were hat-tricks against Batley at Thrum Hall and at Doncaster. Amazingly, he thus became the first Halifax half-back to score two hat-tricks in a season since Ned Rees in 1913/14.

Halifax won promotion in 1973/74, Sammy scoring 4 tries and 2 goals in 22 outings, but were relegated in 1974/75, when he made 31 appearances in a horrendous campaign. He did manage to create one piece of history, however, on 23 February 1975 in a 13-12 home victory over Bramley, when he kicked the first one-point drop goal for the club.

Sammy was exchanged for Wakefield Trinity's Joe Bonnar and spent two years at Belle Vue before moving to Leeds. He enjoyed a golden period with the Loiners, playing at Wembley in 1978, when St Helens were beaten 14-12, while in 1979 he figured at stand-off in Leeds's 24-2 demolition of Bradford Northern in the Premiership final at Fartown. He was also a Yorkshire Cup-winner when Leeds beat Halifax later in 1979.

# Derrick Schofield
Second-row forward, 1953-1956

**Previous club:** Rochdale Hornets

**Halifax debut:** 26 September 1953
 *v.* St Helens

**Final Halifax appearance:** 27 October 1956
 *v.* Bradford Northern

**Appearances:** 111

**Tries:** 32   **Goals:** 10   **Points:** 116

**Transferred to:** Castleford

**Honours:** Lancashire, England, Great Britain

There were few finer sights in rugby league in the 1950s than Derrick Schofield crashing through the middle of the field on surging runs, causing havoc in opposing defences. Derrick, often scrum-capped, was an extremely athletic second-rower with the speed, habits and instincts of a three-quarter, despite being a six-foot, fourteen-and-a-half-stone forward. He was a good handler and one of those forwards who could make a difference. He was a fair goal-kicker too.

Derrick, a Rochdalian, had been a junior England International (Under-21s) winger in 1949. He had joined Rochdale Hornets straight from the Army and played much of his rugby for them in the three-quarters, amassing 21 tries and 103 goals in 114 games. Despite Hornets' lowly status he had risen to such prominence that Lancashire, England and Great Britain had all honoured him in the 1952/53 campaign.

Halifax signed him on 24 September 1953, £3,000 (plus centre Dennis Bradley) making it an expensive deal for the club. Derrick was required to add that extra zip to what was already arguably the most powerful pack in the league. He certainly provided the goods on his debut two days later when champions St Helens were beaten 14-3 at Thrum Hall and he scored his first try for the club in his third game, a record 40-10 victory at Leeds.

Derrick was a try-scorer in the Challenge Cup semi-final victory over Hunslet in 1954 and played in all the games against Warrington at Wembley, Odsal and Maine Road. His only winners' medal for the season, however, was for the Yorkshire League Championship. In 36 games he scored 5 tries but got another in Belfast, where Halifax beat Warrington 34-15 in an exhibition match.

In 1954/55 Halifax won the Yorkshire Cup beating Hull but Derrick only played in the semi-final against Leeds. The following season he made up for that, playing in the final and replay, when Hull were again beaten. He also earned a second Yorkshire League winners' medal. That 1955/56 season saw him break all records for a Halifax forward as he ran in 17 tries, including three in a 34-0 home win over Huddersfield. He was, however, surprisingly left out of the team for the Challenge Cup final. He was restored to favour the following week for the Championship final against Hull, who beat Halifax 10-9.

Despite playing for Great Britain against New Zealand and France in 1955/56, Derrick was transferred to Castleford in November 1956, subsequently joining Rochdale and, finally, Dewsbury. Among his last games for Halifax were a couple at full-back and one on the right wing against Salford, when he bagged two tries. In 1962 he retired but not before he had captained Dewsbury to a famous 5-3 first round Challenge Cup-tie victory over Halifax at Crown Flatt.

# John Schuster

Right-centre, 1993-1997

**Previous club:** Newcastle Knights

**Halifax debut:** 29 August 1993 v. Oldham

**Final Halifax appearance:** 7 September 1997
   v. Castleford

**Appearances:** 116 + 1 sub

**Tries:** 50   **Goals:** 404 + 5 drop goals

**Points:** 1,013

**Transferred to:** Blackheath RU

**Honours:** Western Samoa

Anyone who saw footage of John Schuster playing rugby union for the All Blacks in 1988 and 1989 knew that he was a natural for rugby league. He had all the skills necessary for a top player. He looked comfortable with the ball in his hands – not always the case with rugby union middle backs. When he turned to league he confirmed that view. As a centre with Halifax John was pure class – a dexterous handler and passer, who was decidedly quicker than he looked with the most exquisite shimmy that left defenders rooted to the spot. He was a frequent try-scorer and had a particularly fruitful association with John Bentley on the right flank. On top of all that, he was one of the best goal-kickers anyone could wish to see. John was a master at not playing the ball with his foot, presaging a practice which seems to have been institutionalised in Super League in 2003!

John was born in Apia, Western Samoa, in 1964 and played in 7 RU Tests as a stand-off for his country before moving to New Zealand, where he won another 10 caps. He turned to rugby league in Australia with Newcastle Knights in 1991, scoring 266 points for them in three seasons before arriving at Thrum Hall in August 1993.

It was not until Paul Bishop was injured in November that John took over the kicking duties and proved hugely successful. His first season brought him 198 points (17 tries, 65 goals) and he only missed one of Halifax's 34 fixtures. The 1994/95 season was a triumph for him. He played in all 34 matches and shattered Colin Whitfield's club record of 298 points set in 1986/87. His tally was 362 points (19 tries, 142 goals, and 2 drop goals) and remains a record to this day (2004). His 128 goals in league matches made him the leading goal-kicker in the First Division, while his 326 points in the league was a record in the top division since the league split in 1973.

The 1994/95 season also saw him become only the second Halifax player in history to play and score in every game in a season. He broke Bruce Burton's club record for points in a match when he amassed 32 (3 tries, 10 goals) in a 72-0 victory at Doncaster. Injuries restricted John to just 12 games in 1995/96 but he still claimed 112 points and captained Western Samoa in the Centenary World Cup.

He was back at full pelt in 1996 with 256 points in 23 appearances. Included were a personal best eleven goals in a home win against Workington Town and ten goals in a stupendous 64-24 butchering of Leeds in the last game of the season.

Season 1997 was his last and was ruined by injury. Nonetheless, he still managed to become the fourth Halifax player to break the 1,000 points barrier, when he scored eleven points in a 28-28 draw at London Broncos on 25 August.

# Mick Scott
Second-row forward, loose forward, 1974-1991

**Previous club:** Siddal ARL (1), Wigan (2),
York (3)

**Halifax debut:** 20 October 1974 v. St Helens

**Final Halifax appearance:** 12 May 1991
v. Salford  Second Division Premiership
final

**Appearances:** 249 + 57 subs

**Tries:** 43   **Goals:** 23 + 20 drop goals

**Points:** 202

**Transferred to:** Wigan (1), York (2)

On 1 July 1974 the *Evening Courier* announced that Halifax had signed Mick Scott, 'an eighteen-year-old loose forward or half-back' from Siddal. It added that he had played for the inter-town team at open age level, had been Man of the Match in the Halifax League Championship final against Keighley Albion and 'can kick goals'. Thirty years later Mick is still at Halifax in a coaching capacity and is truly a local boy made good. He never did play half-back for Halifax but did become one of the best second-row men of his generation. In 1999 he was admitted to the Halifax Hall of Fame and is the last Halifax player to have registered 300 appearances for the club.

From being a long-haired adolescent 'A' teamer to a crew-cut Wembley winner, Mick ('Scotty') has done it all, both on the field and off it, with Halifax. He has coached the Academy, the 'A' team and briefly the firsts, been club captain and manager of the club lottery, the 'Fax Flyer'. On the field he was an inspiration, always giving of his best, a model of consistency. An intelligent ball player, tremendously hard-working defender, creative on attack with a fine ability to read the game, Mick has also been a match-winner with his ability to drop goals, to score crucial tries and to make them for others. Mick could be relied on to take the right option in any given situation and he was one of those players who was sorely missed when absent from the team.

The great mystery about Mick Scott was how the representative selectors failed to recognise his myriad talents.

Mick joined Halifax at one of the lowest points of the club's history. In his 'A' team debut as loose forward at Hull KR on 24 August 1974, he kicked a goal in a 2-38 loss. It was worse on his first-team debut against St Helens at Thrum Hall, when he was a thirteenth-minute substitute for David Briggs. Halifax lost 15-47, the most points they had ever conceded at home in the league. Mick's talent was, however, unmistakeable and in his first season he made 23 appearances, mostly in the second row. In 1975/76 he reverted to loose forward but was back in the second row for 1976/77 when he won the Player of the Year award, appearing in 28 games and scoring 4 tries and 12 goals, including a match-winning drop against Whitehaven.

In 1977/78 Mick played in the team which lost to Cawoods and finished bottom of the league but thereafter it was all onwards and

*Wembley 1987. Mick Scott prepares to pass to Gary Stephens as Andy Platt approaches.*

upwards. The following season he played in his first semi-final, when York won 4-2 at Thrum Hall in the Yorkshire Cup. The 1979/80 season saw him in prime form as Halifax won promotion, reached the Yorkshire Cup final and the semi-finals of the Challenge Cup. He won the inaugural Tetley Trophy for the club's most consistent player and was the top forward try-scorer with a dozen. Fans who recall this era will have fond and vivid memories of Mick finishing off sublime set moves involving Kenny Loxton and Dave Callon.

Mick played magnificently in a Halifax team which was agonisingly unfortunate to be relegated in 1980/81. He was the club's leading try-scorer with 13 and also landed 13 goals, 11 of which were dropped, including three in a home victory over Barrow. In seven seasons he had made 176 appearances, in which he had claimed 174 points (36 tries, 43 goals). He was certainly too good for the Second Division but it was no recompense to the Halifax fans when he signed for Wigan for £28,500 at the start of the 1981/82 season.

He enjoyed four successful seasons at Wigan, making 125 appearances (12 tries) and appearing at Wembley in 1984. Wigan also won the Challenge Cup in 1985, Mick playing in the semi-final but not the final, and he was a winner in the Players Trophy final in 1982/83, while he also gained a runners-up medal for the Lancashire Cup in 1984.

Mick was coming up to thirty in the summer of 1985 and was a publican in Mixenden. It made good sense for him to return to his hometown club and Halifax got a bargain when he was re-signed for £9,000. He made his reappearance in the second row alongside debutant Paul Dixon in a 12-12 home draw against Oldham on 1 September 1985. He proved to be a tower of strength, playing in 32 games as Halifax swept to the Championship. He was runner-up in the Player of the Year awards and ended the season playing at blind-side prop in the Premiership final in Cavil Heugh's absence. In 1986/87 he began by picking up a winners medal when Halifax beat Castleford in the Charity Shield on the Isle of Man and ended it with another at Wembley as St Helens were beaten 19-18.

He was back at Wembley in 1988, substituting for the injured Les Holliday after twenty minutes, but had to settle for a runners-up medal as Wigan walloped 'Fax 32-12. In January 1989 Mick briefly joined York, playing 9 games, before returning a third time to Thrum Hall for the 1989/90 season as assistant coach to John Dorahy. Mick ended up playing in 15 games, including the Regal Trophy final against Wigan, having been a try-scorer in 'Fax's sensational semi-final victory over St Helens.

Season 1990/91 was his swansong. He was appointed captain, led the team against the Australians but later gave up the leadership to Brendan Hill. He still put in 32 appearances as Halifax won promotion and came off the bench to replace Peter Bell in the Second Division Premiership final against Salford.

# Jack Scroby

Second-row forward, prop, 1959-1970

**Previous club:** Bradford Northern

**Halifax debut:** 29 August 1959 v. Wakefield Trinity Yorkshire Cup

**Final Halifax appearance:** 28 February 1970 v. Hunslet

**Appearances:** 311 + 4 subs

**Tries:** 22    **Goals:** 0    **Points:** 66

**Transferred to:** Huddersfield

**Honours:** Yorkshire

All rugby league clubs make mistakes and all have been guilty of letting promising local players slip through their fingers. Halifax made one such mistake with Jack Scroby, but rectified it at considerable expense.

Jack was a local, who played rugby union at Crossley and Porter Grammar School, and amateur rugby league for Siddal and Ovenden before being signed by Bradford Northern, ironically when their manager was Dai Rees, captain of Halifax's 1931 Challenge Cup-winning team. Jack made his debut in first-class rugby league at second row in Northern's 23-8 victory at Liverpool City on 20 August 1955. His usual position at Odsal was, however, loose forward, figuring there in 73 of his 104 games for the club. He scored 16 tries for Bradford and a solitary goal, when Wakefield Trinity were beaten 11-10 at Odsal on 19 October 1957.

There were no winners' medals or caps while he played for Bradford but he did gain experience and figured in their clash with the Australians in 1956 and in a Yorkshire Cup semi-final against York in 1957. His talents were, however, obvious and there was much interest in him from other clubs. Halifax were the lucky club but his signature cost a club record £7,500 and was at the time (1959) one of the biggest transfer fees ever paid.

When he joined Halifax Jack was in the Army, serving with the Duke of Wellington's Regiment in Northern Ireland. He had the distinction of representing the Army against the Navy and the RAF at Twickenham in 1959, although both games were lost.

Jack's debut for Halifax was a tremendous first-round Yorkshire Cup-tie in which Wakefield Trinity were beaten 17-14. It was the first game at Thrum Hall to be televised. Jack began his Halifax career in the second-row alongside Brian Sparks. For the first few years Jack played predominantly in the second row for 'Fax, turning out only 8 times at loose forward, including the fixture against the 1959 Kangaroos, and occasionally at prop.

In 1960/61 Jack appeared in Halifax's 12-18 loss against the New Zealand World Cup team and was a tower of strength as Halifax fought their way through to the Challenge Cup semi-finals. Unfortunately, Halifax lost 10-19 to Wigan at Swinton, Jack scoring a rare try. It was the nearest he would come to appearing at Wembley. The season did, however, present Jack with his first cap for Yorkshire, although a 19-43 defeat against Cumberland at Whitehaven on 14 September 1960 was a poor start. Jack went on to play 6 games for Yorkshire between 1960 and 1968, 5 of them against Cumberland and a Roses Match at Headingley in 1966, when the floodlights were inaugurated.

Halifax were not a successful team in the early 1960s but the nucleus of a good side was beginning to form. Jack saw the glimmerings of more productive times ahead when 'Fax qualified for the new First Division in 1962/63 and reached the semi-finals of the Yorkshire Cup and Eastern Division Championships that season. The breakthrough came in

*Jack Scroby crashes over for a rare try against Doncaster in 1966. Gordon Baker, Ronnie James and Terry Fogerty (on ground) look on. Doncaster winger Peter Goodchild, on the extreme right, later joined Halifax and is featured as one of the 100 Great Thrum Hallers.*

1963/64, the season in which Jack moved permanently into the front row. He was at blind-side prop when Halifax won the Yorkshire Cup, beating Featherstone Rovers 10-0 at Belle Vue, Wakefield, but missed the win over Castleford at Fartown in the Eastern Division Championship final through injury.

That injury kept Jack out of the side until October 1964, when he returned to play in 31 of Halifax's remaining 32 fixtures, culminating in Halifax's winning of the Championship in May 1965. Jack was a cornerstone of a classic pack – Ken Roberts, Dave Harrison (or Stuart Kelley), Jack Scroby, Colin Dixon, Terry Fogerty and Charlie Renilson. Jack was not its most spectacular member but he was indispensable. He was a big man – over sixteen stones – who knew how to use his weight and strength in the scrums. He was a tireless tackler and a prodigious worker. He was a safe handler, who could use the ball to advantage, and he was one of those forwards who wore down the opposition. Tellingly, because of all his unspectacular graft, Jack was the type of player who was most noticed by his absence.

The 1964/65 season brought Jack 4 tries.

Two were exceptionally important and effectively won Halifax three crucial league points. On 9 January 1965 he scored Halifax's only try in a mudbath at Thrum Hall enabling them to salvage a 5-5 draw against Widnes, while on 27 March his try, the only one of the game, won 'Fax's match at Keighley 9-8. In the Championship final victory over St Helens Jack played a blinder as the Halifax forwards dictated the play.

In 1965/66 Jack played in 37 games, including the fixture against New Zealand and in all the play-off matches, scoring in a 21-7 victory at Bradford but this time he had to be content with a Championship runners-up medal. It was something of a let-down that Jack was not selected for the 1966 Lions tour. He did, however, play against the Lions for a Rest of the League XIII at Headingley on their return from Australasia.

Jack continued until 1970 when he left to coach Huddersfield. In later years Jack contributed to Halifax's cause, coaching at various levels – he was Chris Anderson's assistant in the '80s – and acting as the club's official time-keeper.

# John Shaw
Hooker, 1958-1965

**Previous club:** Wakefield Trinity

**Halifax debut:** 8 November 1958 v. Hull Kingston Rovers

**Final Halifax appearance:** 6 April 1965 v. Dewsbury

**Appearances:** 166 + 1 sub

**Tries:** 12   **Goals:** 0   **Points:** 36

**Transferred to:** Hull Kingston Rovers

**Honours:** Yorkshire, Great Britain

When Alvin Ackerley's long and successful hooking reign at Thrum Hall ended in 1958, Halifax signed John 'Joby' Shaw from Wakefield Trinity for £2,100. John was already an experienced number nine, who had just helped Yorkshire to win the County Championship and had seven years in the first team and almost 200 appearances for Wakefield behind him. He was an ideal replacement for Ackerley. Chunky and weighing fourteen stones, John had few peers in the art of winning ball possession and he was a frequent and damaging tackler, who relished the hardest of struggles. The hazards of the hooking role were well known to John – injuries, dismissals and suspensions. Consequently, the longest run of consecutive appearances he mustered for Halifax was only seventeen but he always came back stronger.

His debut for Halifax, a 22-13 victory over Hull KR, saw him propped by veteran internationals John Thorley and Jack Wilkinson but he was soon left with youngsters Frank Fox and Roger Crabtree. Injury and dispute blighted the 1959/60 season for him but the following season saw him in prime form. He regained his Yorkshire place and won a spot in Great Britain's World Cup squad. He took over at hooker from the great Tommy Harris for the second game of the tournament against France at Swinton and retained the job in the decider against Australia at Odsal. In a brutal encounter John outhooked Noel Kelly 16-13 as Britain took

the trophy with a 10-3 triumph.

He was Britain's hooker in two more victorious tests against France in 1960/61. He finished the season with five tries for Halifax, equalling Mel Meek's post-war record for a hooker. Surprisingly, John never played at Wembley but came as near as he ever did during 1960/61, playing in Halifax's 10-19 loss to Wigan in the Cup semi-final.

In 1961/62 he played for Halifax-Huddersfield combined XIII against the New Zealanders and helped Halifax qualify for the new First Division. At the end of the campaign, aged twenty-eight, he toured Australasia as a Lion, appearing in the last test against New Zealand.

The 1963/64 season brought more honours and medals. He was restored to the Yorkshire team, playing alongside Frank Fox against Cumberland, at Wakefield, and the Australians, the latter producing a famous 11-5 victory at Craven Park, Hull. There was considerable success too with the Thrum Hallers, as he appeared in both the 10-0 Yorkshire Cup final victory over Featherstone Rovers and the 20-12 win against Castleford in the Eastern Division Championship final.

His last season at Thrum Hall brought Halifax their first Championship since 1906/07 but John only played in six matches as Stuart Kelley and the newly signed Dave Harrison from St Helens superseded him.

# Steve Smith

Full-back, 1982-1992

**Previous club:** Halifax Colts

**Halifax debut:** 10 October 1982 v. Barrow

**Final Halifax appearance:** 16 February 1992
v. Swinton

**Appearances:** 163 + 28 subs

**Tries:** 36  **Goals:** 112  **Points:** 366

**Transferred to:** Batley

Steve Smith was a top class full-back and a loyal clubman, who probably did not reap his due rewards. Circumstances seemed to conspire against him but he always bounced back and won the respect of a generation of Halifax fans, entertaining them for a decade.

A product of Batley Boys, he had trials with Batley, who somehow contrived to fail to sign him. He ended up playing for Keighley Colts, who were taken over by Halifax, and he signed for the club on 27 August 1981. Within six months he had won a first-team place, going on to make 25 appearances in 1982/83. Steve had just about all the attributes necessary for full-back and he was also quick and determined enough to turn out on the wing on 20 occasions. He was extremely sound in defence, strong in the tackle, a fine catcher and returner of the ball and excellent at reading the game. In attack he was brave, direct and hard to tackle. He could kick goals and, importantly, he was consistent and cool under pressure.

In 1983/84 he was Halifax's Player of the Year, as the team won promotion. He displayed his attacking skills with a hat-trick from full-back, a rare achievement, in a 34-18 win at Keighley, and in the last game of the

season potted 22 points (7 goals, 2 tries) in a 50-9 home win against Rochdale Hornets.

He was certainly First Division class and a possibility for honours. Unfortunately, he broke his ankle at Featherstone on 21 October 1984 and missed a big proportion of the season. In 1985/86 Halifax brought over Joe Kilroy to play full-back. Even so, Steve played in 23 games, mostly on the wing, top-scored with 82 points, and gave several match-winning performances. He was rewarded with a Championship-winners' medal and a place as substitute in the Premiership final.

Halifax replaced Kilroy with Graham Eadie in 1986/87, so Steve had to be satisfied with a winning Charity Shield appearance against Castleford and a game against the Kangaroos. He missed out on both of Halifax's Wembley appearances in 1987 and 1988, winning the 'A' team Player of the Year award in 1987/88. Steve only played 8 games in the relegation season of 1988/89 but was back in favour the following season, appearing in Halifax's gallant defeat by Wigan in the Regal Trophy final. He also had the great distinction of winning the James Harrison Trophy in 1989/90, emulating Halifax icons Garfield Owen, Charlie Renilson and Jack Scroby.

1990/91, his last full season, brought promotion, another appearance against the Kangaroos and a Second Division Premiership runners-up medal after Halifax's loss to Salford at Old Trafford. He made the most appearances of his career in that final season – 32, in which he scored 64 points. Steve was awarded a well-deserved benefit in 1991.

# Alan Snowden
Right-winger, 1958-1962

**Previous club:** Hunslet

**Halifax debut:** 18 January 1958 v. Hull Kingston Rovers

**Final Halifax appearance:** 6 January 1962 v. Whitehaven

**Appearances:** 129

**Tries:** 63   **Goals:** 0   **Points:** 189

**Transferred to:** Retired

**Honours:** Yorkshire

Halifax knew just what they were getting when they spent £2,000 on Hunslet's Alan Snowden in January 1958. He had been recruited in response to the serious injury which had just put Johnny Freeman out of the game for a year. Alan was a tremendously hard-running right-wingman, who had a nice line in beating full-backs with a sudden inside step as they tried to take him into touch. He was also a past master in the dying art of the flying cross-kick, which often resulted in tries for his fellow wingmen.

Even in an age when wingers were real fliers, Alan Snowden stood out for his pace. His career with Hunslet had yielded him 151 tries in 213 appearances between 1950 and 1958. He had set a club record with 34 tries in 1956/57 and had topped the Hunslet try-scorers for five consecutive seasons prior to arriving at Thrum Hall.

His first game was sensational for he ran over for four tries in Halifax's 28-7 home victory over Hull KR, a debut without precedent at the club. Alan quickly formed a potent right-wing combination with John Burnett. He picked up a Yorkshire League Championship winners' medal for 1957/58, his only winners' medal. In 1958/59, his first full season at Halifax, Alan bagged 26 tries, while Burnett scored 27. Among Alan's total were another haul of four in a 33-17 win against Dewsbury and, possibly, one of the greatest individual tries ever scored at Thrum Hall – a stunning effort almost from his own line against St Helens.

In 1959/60 Alan captained Halifax, an unusual job for a winger in any era. He was captain when Halifax lost 5-17 to the 1959 Australians and the following year played against the New Zealand World Cup team which beat Halifax 18-12. Unfortunately, he missed two of the biggest games played by Halifax in his time – both against Wigan. Injury kept him out of the third-round Challenge Cup-tie in 1959, which attracted Halifax's biggest ever crowd (29,153) and he also missed the Challenge Cup semi-final in 1961. He had been unlucky at Hunslet too, missing their Yorkshire Cup final appearance in 1956 and their Challenge Cup semi-final against Halifax in 1954, while he tasted defeat against Barrow at the same stage in 1955.

Alan played for Yorkshire once while at Hunslet and won four more county caps while at Halifax, all in combination with John Burnett. He picked up County Championship medals for 1957/58 and 1958/59, scoring tries in three of his five appearances.

A native of Leeds, Alan played rugby league as a youth for Burley National but signed for Hunslet for £500 from Roundhay RU club. He later became production manager at the *Halifax Courier*, which for four years chronicled his Thrum Hall feats.

# Roy Southernwood

Scrum-half, number nine, 1990-1996

**Previous club:** Castleford

**Halifax debut:** 26 August 1990 v. Doncaster
Yorkshire Cup

**Final Halifax appearance:** 12 April 1996
v. Warrington

**Appearances:** 142 + 7 subs

**Tries:** 20   **Goals:** 1 drop goal   **Points:** 81

**Transferred to:** Wakefield Trinity

**Honours:** Great Britain Colts, Great Britain
Under-21s

Roy ('Jockey') Southernwood had a meritorious career before he joined Halifax, aged twenty-two, on 24 August 1990. Castleford had signed him from Travellers Saints in 1985. In 1986/87 Roy had captained Yorkshire and Great Britain Colts, having played for Castleford first team the previous season. In 1987 he appeared in the Yorkshire Cup final at scrum-half to John Joyner in a 12-12 draw against Bradford Northern at Headingley. In the replay at Elland Road he played stand-off to Bob Beardmore but Cas lost 2-11. In 1989 he represented Great Britain Under-21s against France at Leeds and Carpentras, captaining on the latter occasion.

Roy made a try-scoring debut for Halifax at stand-off, as partner to John Lyons but was quickly moved to scrum-half. For most of his initial season he played alongside the enigmatic and abrasive Jimmy Irvine. Martin Wood partnered him when Halifax gave the Australians a rare tussle before losing 18-36 and Lyons was his partner at Old Trafford, when Salford beat 'Fax in the Second Division Premiership final. Roy played 35 games (9 tries) in that promotion season.

Halifax brought in Paul Harkin as scrum-half and captain for 1991/92 and Roger Millward elected to follow the vogue of playing half-backs at number nine. Roy seemed at home in the front row, despite his

5' 7" frame, and his half-back career effectively ended. Only one of his 114 further games as a Thrum Haller was at scrum-half.

Roy proved a real beaver in his new role and when the ten-metre law was introduced in 1992 it suited him perfectly. He was a constant menace at the rucks, scurrying away from the play-the-balls before releasing the ball to his supports. He was a terrier in the tackle too and, when he was absent from the team, his organising, tackling and reliability were missed. Of course, Roy was fortunate in having such huskies as Karl Harrison, Brendan Hill, Peter Bell, John Fieldhouse and Adam Fogerty alongside him, even if genuine hooking was no longer required.

In his time at Thrum Hall Halifax won no trophies and the nearest Roy came to Wembley was three third-round cup-ties, the most notable being the excruciating last-gasp 18-19 loss to Wigan at a snowy Thrum Hall in 1993. By 1995/96 his days were numbered with the arrival of Paul Rowley and his last big game for Halifax was in the Premiership play-off at St Helens in 1995. He continued to give good service, however, in the Alliance team before leaving for Wakefield Trinity in 1997.

It was with Wakefield that Roy finally earned a tangible reward after so much endeavour. Trinity finished top of the First Division and beat Featherstone Rovers 24-22 in the Grand Final. Roy opened the scoring with a second-minute try.

# Brian Sparks

Second-row forward, 1957-1961

**Previous club:** Neath RU

**Halifax debut:** 28 December 1957 v. Hunslet

**Final Halifax appearance:** 29 April 1961
   v. Salford

**Appearances:** 115

**Tries:** 17   **Goals:** 0   **Points:** 51

**Transferred to:** Salford

A hard-working, hard-running back-rower, who appeared happiest when in the thick of things, Brian Sparks had a relatively short career at Thrum Hall. Distinguished by his crew-cut hair, sometimes covered by a scrum cap, Brian was also unlucky when it came to winning things, at least in rugby league.

His rugby union career was distinguished, to say the least. Born in Llanharan, a prolific producer of fine Welsh players, Brian captained Cowbridge Grammar School before playing club rugby for Pontypool, Bridgend and Neath. He also played county rugby for Glamorgan and Devon, being a member of the Devon XV which beat Yorkshire in the County Championship final of 1957. He played for Glamorgan Police but then changed professions to become a teacher, captaining St Luke's College, Exeter, to victory in the 1957 Middlesex Sevens. He won 7 Wales RU caps (1954-57) as a flanker and represented the Barbarians.

Late in 1957 he joined Halifax for £1,800, becoming the seventh and last Welsh RU cap to sign for the club. He came to the club at a time when the team was in decline and although they won the Yorkshire League in 1957/58, he missed winning a medal as he only played in five Yorkshire League games. From the start of his league career Brian was a fixture in the Halifax second-row, his first partners being Alan Jarman and, occasionally, Jack Wilkinson. He scored a try on his debut, a 36-3 home victory over Hunslet.

In 1958/59, when he topped the Halifax forwards try-scoring with 7, he had the pleasure and pain of playing before Thrum Hall's record crowd – over 29,000 – but losing 0-26 to Wigan. He was also selected, with Garfield Owen and John Thorley, for a Welsh XIII against France at Toulouse but was unable to play.

In 1959/60 he played in losing teams against the Australians (5-17) and against Hull (9-18) at The Boulevard in the Yorkshire Cup semi-final. He played loose forward ten times that season but established a formidable second-row partnership with newly signed Jack Scroby.

Brian, 5' 10.5" and 13st 12lbs, was made captain in 1960/61, succeeding Alan Snowden, and he proved a good leader in what turned out to be his last season. Halifax swept through to the semi-final of the Challenge Cup but Brian's hopes of leading them out at Wembley disappeared when Wigan beat them 19-10 at Swinton. He only played four more games for the club before retiring and returning to Wales.

He did, however, join Salford in October 1964, aged thirty-three, and played just over a year for them, making 37 appearances (2 tries) before retiring for good. Brian became a head teacher and in 1963 was founder chairman of the Welsh Schools Basketball Association.

# George Standidge

Blind-side prop, 1980-1982

**Previous club:** Hunslet

**Halifax debut:** 5 October 1980 *v.*
    Featherstone Rovers

**Final Halifax appearance:** 7 May 1982
    *v.* Doncaster

**Appearances:** 54 + 2 subs

**Tries:** 13    **Goals:** 0    **Points:** 39

**Transferred to:** Rochdale Hornets

**Honours:** Yorkshire

It is fair to say that George Standidge – the idol of the Scratching Shed – was as near to a cult figure as makes no difference during his two-season spell at Thrum Hall.

When George was signed by Halifax from Hunslet in October 1980 his transfer fee was £6,000. That was a lot of money for a prop forward who, however, had a wealth of experience from ten years and close on 250 games with Batley, Bramley and Hunslet, when they were called New Hunslet. George had been a member of New Hunslet promotion-winning sides in 1976/77 and 1978/79 but otherwise had won no caps or medals. He had started his career as an amateur with Shaw Cross.

He joined a Halifax team which had just been promoted and had made a horrendous start to the season, losing seven of the opening eight league fixtures. It was going to be uphill all the way. George was a hit from the start, scoring a typical piledriving try on his debut, a 14-24 defeat at Featherstone Rovers. Ten wins from the remaining twenty-one league matches almost kept Halifax in the top division, as Mick Blacker's side made up for what it lacked in class and pace with skill, spirit and sheer bloody-mindedness.

At the heart of the team was George, who had arrived at Thrum Hall just as another absolute hero of the fans, Alan Wood, departed. George simply took over Woody's

mantle. Although not the biggest of forwards, George appeared to have eaten a lot of spinach, for when he drove into the massed ranks of opposing packs all hell seemed to be let loose. It was reminiscent of Popeye. Bodies flew in all directions, as George refused to be brought down. In that first season George scored 8 tries in 29 games, all greeted with rapture by the fans, as the stocky prop rose smiling and waving after securing the touchdowns. He had a real rapport with the supporters. Besides his proclivity for blockbusting runs, George was a strong defender, a tough scrummager and his handling skills were good enough to provide others with opportunities.

The 1981/82 season saw Halifax win promotion, George contributing another 5 tries in 27 barnstorming outings and forming a powerful front row with Nigel Whitehouse and Alan Ackroyd. George was finally rewarded with a county cap, when Yorkshire called him up for the Championship decider against Cumberland at Whitehaven on 23 September 1981, when his co-prop was another future Thrum Hall favourite Roy Dickinson. His last appearance for Halifax came in a 32-5 home beating of Doncaster, when Ken Loxton, Tony Garforth and Dave Cholmondeley also made their finales.

Typically, on leaving the club, George wrote a letter to the *Evening Courier* explaining his decision and thanking the Halifax fans – possibly a unique occurrence.

# Gary Stephens
Scrum-half, 1985-1987

**Previous club:** Leigh

**Halifax debut:** 1 September 1985 v. Oldham

**Final Halifax appearance:** 11 October 1987
   v. Bradford Northern

**Appearances:** 82

**Tries:** 17   **Goals:** 9 drop goals   **Points:** 77

**Transferred to:** York

**Honours:** Yorkshire, England, Great Britain

Gary Stephens had been in the game a long time when he arrived at Thrum Hall in 1985. He had spent most of his career (1969-80) with his native Castleford, earning winners' medals for the Yorkshire Cup, Floodlit Trophy and John Player Trophy and enjoying a benefit with Phil Johnson. He had subsequently played with Wigan, losing at Wembley in 1984, Warrington and Leigh, while in 1976 and 1977 he had played in Australia with Manly, winning the Grand Final with a Man of the Match performance in 1976. He had captained Yorkshire, played for England, won 5 Test caps and toured with the Lions in 1979.

He was thirty-three when he made his debut for Halifax in a 12-12 draw with Oldham at Thrum Hall, partnering another old 'un in player-coach Chris Anderson. If anyone thought Gary, all 5' 5" and perhaps eleven stones of him, was past it they were mistaken. True, he did not tackle himself to a standstill. That was not his job. He was there to organise, to provide the ammunition for others. He was a busy, probing irritant to opponents, a master of the short pass, which sent the likes of Geoff Robinson, Paul Dixon and Graham Eadie over for tries or away on rampaging runs. He worked the scrums well, took the right options, had a good kicking game and was adept at dropping goals.

He proved his durability by playing in all thirty-seven of Halifax's games in his debut season and extended that run to 55 consecutive appearances the following season.

In 1985/86 Halifax took the Championship with Gary playing a leading role in his combination with Anderson. He scored 8 tries, made countless others and dropped 7 goals – all the goals dropped by Halifax during the season. He also earned a Premiership runners-up medal when Halifax went down to Warrington in the final at Elland Road.

At the start of the 1986/87 campaign he had the satisfaction of being in the team which beat his original side Castleford 9-8 in the Charity Shield on the Isle of Man. That was, however, eclipsed when Halifax fought their way through to Wembley and that sensational 19-18 victory over St Helens. In the twilight of his career Gary had finally won the two major domestic honours which had eluded him – a Championship winners' and a Challenge Cup winners' medal.

Gary remained at Halifax for only five more months after Wembley, appearing in another Charity Shield match on the Isle of Man, when Halifax lost heavily to Wigan. He was succeeded in the Halifax number seven jersey by Steve Robinson. Gary briefly went on loan to Leeds but eventually became player-coach with York. In later years he returned to Halifax as a member of the coaching staff.

**Previous club:** Neath RU

**Halifax debut:** 12 April 1952 v. St Helens

**Final Halifax appearance:** 16 January 1960
v. Hunslet

**Appearances:** 262

**Tries:** 27   **Goals:** 0   **Points:** 81

**Transferred to:** Dewsbury

**Honours:** Rugby League XIII, Wales, Other
Nationalities, Great Britain

John Thorley came to Halifax as a second-row forward but made his reputation as an open-side prop who won many of the game's highest honours. A Welsh rugby union international trialist in 1950/51, John cost Halifax £1,350 after playing a couple of games as an unnamed trialist at St Helens and Oldham in April 1952. After making half-a-dozen appearances in the second row, his first outing at number eight in a 5-3 win at Featherstone on 31 January 1953 left no one in any doubt as to where he should play. John, Alvin Ackerley and Jack Wilkinson were arguably as effective a front row as ever played rugby league.

A six-foot, fourteen-and-a-half-stone solid block of humanity, John was one of the most formidable scrummagers of his era, a good tackler and, with 27 tries for 'Fax, a prolific scorer for a prop. He was extremely durable, as his feat of playing in forty or more matches in a season four times clearly demonstrates. In 1953/54 John played 45 games for Halifax, including the Challenge Cup final, the Odsal Replay and the Championship final, all against Warrington, scoring the only try of the match in the latter at Maine Road. Although Halifax gained only runners-up medals for the Cup and Championship, John did gain a Yorkshire League Championship winners' medal. The 1953/54 season also saw him win caps for Wales against Other Nationalities and France.

On 23 October 1954 John was in the Halifax front row when Hull were beaten 22-14 at Headingley in the Yorkshire Cup final. A week later he was in France, a leading light in Great Britain's surprise winning of the inaugural rugby league World Cup, figuring in all four of Britain's games. At the close of the season he was back in France playing for a Welsh XIII against France 'B' at Nantes.

In 1955/56 he represented Other Nationalities, along with Tommy Lynch, in crushing victories over France and England – the other Nats' last games. He played in other representative fixtures for a Rugby League XIII versus New Zealand and for Britain against France during the season. Domestically he earned Yorkshire Cup and Yorkshire League-winners' medals and played in Halifax's Championship final defeat by Hull but was left out of the Challenge Cup final team against St Helens, when his scrummaging expertise was sorely missed.

John set a record for the club in 1956/57, which will probably never be beaten, by playing in 48 of Halifax's 49 fixtures, among them a 6-3 victory over the Australians – he had also played in 'Fax's 18-17 win over the 1955 Kiwis – and all four of Halifax's European Championship matches against Albi and Carcassonne. As late as the 1958/59 season John was still topping the club appearances lists with 40 games and appearing for a Welsh XIII in France.

# Peter Todd

Centre, utility back, 1950-1955

**Previous club:** Salford

**Halifax debut:** 25 November 1950 v. Bramley

**Final Halifax appearance:** 1 October 1955
    v. Castleford

**Appearances:** 119

**Tries:** 38   **Goals:** 0   **Points:** 114

**Transferred to:** Dewsbury

Peter Todd came from good rugby league stock. His father, George, was a member of the fabulous Huddersfield Team of All the Talents before and after the First World War, playing on the wing in several major finals in a three-quarter line which included such immortals as Harold Wagstaff, Albert Rosenfeld and Stanley Moorhouse. Peter's brother Harry also played as a winger with Huddersfield and Liverpool Stanley.

After a short time at Fartown, Peter joined Salford and was a regular first teamer there for five years (1945/50), playing 142 games and claiming 38 tries. Halifax signed him for £875 in November 1950. 'Fax hammered Bramley 35-10 at Thrum Hall on his debut. He played at left-centre and the Halifax three-quarters – three Welshmen – ran in seven tries, Peter being the only one not to score. That was rectified a few games later when he bagged a hat-trick in a 31-0 victory over Castleford.

Scoring tries was not Peter's forte. His strength was his merciless defence, even though he was not particularly big at 5' 10.5" and 12st 3lbs. Few opponents relished coming up against Peter, who would hit hard and often. He was also an extremely versatile performer and played effectively for Halifax in all the back positions except scrum-half.

In his first two seasons at Thrum Hall Peter found it difficult to gain a regular spot, the highlight of this period for him being his appearance at full-back in Halifax's 18-12 defeat of the Kiwis in 1951. By the 1952/53 season he was more established but was still having to fight hard for the centre position alongside Tommy Lynch, his main rivals

being Martin Creeney and Dennis Bradley. In 1952 he played in Halifax's Yorkshire Cup semi-final defeat by Huddersfield but Creeney was preferred as the season wore on and Peter missed out on an appearance in the 1953 Championship final, despite having filled in every position from one to six. He did, however, earn a Yorkshire League Championship winners' medal.

In 1953/54 he won a second Yorkshire League medal and was a big factor in Halifax's progression to the finals of the Challenge Cup and Championship, playing against Warrington at Wembley and Maine Road. He sustained an injury at Wembley which prevented him from appearing in the Odsal replay, Billy Mather taking his place. Peter also played in the two subsequent exhibition games against Warrington in Belfast and Dublin. He had his best season as a try-scorer with 13 in 38 appearances.

In 1954/55 Peter was a member of the team which beat Hull in the Yorkshire Cup final and scored 9 tries in 33 games. His last major game for Halifax was the Championship semi-final defeat at Warrington in 1955, when he was played on the left wing. Peter later went on to captain Dewsbury.

# Ken Traill
Loose forward, 1955-1957

**Previous club:** Bradford Northern

**Halifax debut:** 29 October 1955
    *v.* Featherstone Rovers

**Final Halifax appearance:** 7 December 1957
    *v.* Wakefield Trinity

**Appearances:** 90

**Tries:** 12  **Goals:** 0  **Points:** 36

**Transferred to:** Wakefield Trinity

**Honours:** Yorkshire, England, Great Britain

Ken Traill was undoubtedly one of the most brilliant loose forwards in the game's history, a rare talent, capable of running or turning a match. Tall and flaxen-haired, Ken was a commanding figure, who could spray out amazingly long, pinpoint passes, work delicate moves with his half-backs, send opposing defences scurrying backwards with prodigious touch-finders and bring down attackers with perfectly timed textbook tackles. In short, he was a paragon of loose forward play.

Ken had begun his professional career with Hunslet as a seventeen-year-old in 1944 and had played against Halifax in both legs of the 1944 Yorkshire Cup final, Halifax winning 14-3 on aggregate. In 1947 he had moved to Bradford Northern, where he enjoyed eight highly successful years, playing in three Yorkshire Cup-winning sides, in two Championship finals and earning a Yorkshire League Championship-winners' medal. He also appeared in two Wembley finals, most notably in 1949 when Northern beat Halifax 12-0. His virtues were recognised by the representative selectors, who awarded him 8 Test caps and Lions tours in 1950 and 1954.

Halifax only had the benefit of Ken's services for three seasons but he left an indelible mark on the team's style of play and a deep impression on the fans. Ken arrived at Thrum Hall for a £2,750 fee in October 1955, when he had just passed his twenty-ninth birthday. Halifax won the Yorkshire Cup four

days after he made his debut but he was cup-tied. He was, however, thought to be the key which would transform Halifax into the game's premier team. He certainly came close. The Halifax pack, already arguably the most powerful in rugby league, was strengthened even further by a player who could provide direction and tactical leadership. The Halifax backs were certainly grateful as 'Fax began to play more expansively.

The 1955/56 season saw Halifax come within touching distance of winning all four cups. The Yorkshire League was added to the Yorkshire Cup and Halifax swept through to the Challenge Cup and Championship finals. Ken played a truly masterful game when 'Fax beat St Helens 23-8 in the Championship semi-final at Thrum Hall. The following week at Wembley St Helens had learned their lesson. Former Halifax forward Alan Prescott clattered Ken in the opening minutes so comprehensively that he was put off his usual game and Halifax lost 2-13 to a late barrage of points. The following week Halifax lost 9-10 to Hull in the Championship final.

Ken was made captain for 1956/57, led Halifax to the semi-final of the Yorkshire Cup but gave up the captaincy to Ken Dean shortly after Halifax's trip to Albi and Carcassonne in November 1956. He won 2 Yorkshire caps during 1956/57 and figured in 44 of Halifax's 49 games. In 1957/58 he earned a Yorkshire League Championship winners' medal but left for Wakefield Trinity for a fee of £1,500.

# Fereti (Freddy) Tuilagi
### Winger, 1995-1998

**Previous club:** Marist St Joseph RU

**Halifax debut:** 5 November 1995 v. St Helens

**Final Halifax appearance:** 4 October 1998
   v. Leeds

**Appearances:** 78 + 4 subs

**Tries:** 34   **Goals:** 0   **Points:** 136

**Transferred to:** St Helens

Freddy Tuilagi scored the first time he handled the ball as a rugby league player, when he touched down after thirty seconds in Halifax's reserve team match against Workington Town 'A' at Thrum Hall. It was a sensational start by any standards but, then, Freddy was a sensational player, who was adored by the fans.

It was thought that he would be a force at centre, and he did play there on seventeen occasions for 'Fax, but he found his true vocation on the wing, even if he did sometimes act more like a forward. Freddy was extremely powerfully built at 5' 11" and 14st 8lb, and when he tackled he went in with every ounce, making opponents very wary as to his whereabouts. On attack he was equally belligerent and took an awful lot of stopping. Freddy was not a length-of-the-field prospect but he was extremely dangerous over fifty or so yards and almost irresistible near the line.

His delight in playing, and particularly in scoring, transmitted itself to the crowd, who revelled in the entertainment he provided. When he arrived he had a 'normal' hair style, progressed to a shaven head and finished with an exotic dreadlocks and beads affair, which in his time at St Helens spawned a Freddy-wigs merchandising boom. Whatever his hairstyle, he never lost his smile.

Freddy had played rugby union for Western Samoa, representing them in World Cups in 1991 in England and 1995 in South Africa. He joined Halifax in September 1995, reuniting with his compatriots Mike Umaga and John Schuster. His first-team debut brought him a try from left wing in a 20-58 loss at St Helens, when his partner was another South Sea Islander, Asa Amone from Tonga. In his first two seasons, he played centre more than winger but suddenly found terrific form as a right-wingman, when his bullocking runs caused havoc. In 1997 he was joint leading try-scorer with Martin Moana on 12 and scored 13 in 1998.

There were no honours for Freddy at Halifax but he did go to Australia in 1997 for the World Club Championship, appearing in the games at Canterbury and Canberra. He was at right wing in the last Halifax team to play at Thrum Hall on 22 March 1998, when Leeds were beaten 35-28 in a friendly.

To the distress of his many Halifax admirers, after the 1998 season Freddy joined St Helens, where he achieved cult status similar to that he had at Thrum Hall. There was plenty of success too, as Saints won the Super League title in 1999 and 2000 and contested the World Club Challenge against Melbourne Storm in 2000, losing the latter heavily, however. After two seasons with Saints, he moved back into rugby union with Leicester Tigers, also making a return to international rugby with Samoa.

# Keith Waites

Left-winger, 1979-1985

**Previous club:** Bramley

**Halifax debut:** 1 April 1979 v. Dewsbury

**Final Halifax appearance:** 1 January 1985 v. Oldham

**Appearances:** 181 + 2 subs

**Tries:** 48   **Goals:** 0   **Points:** 163

**Transferred to:** Retired (went on loan to Hunslet, 1985/86)

A former Stanningley Juniors player, Keith Waites joined Bramley in 1973 as a twenty-year-old winger. He had played under Maurice Bamford with both clubs and joined him at a third, when Halifax signed him in exchange for prop Steve Grinhaff in March 1979.

Leeds-born Keith played over 80 games for Bramley and scored 20 tries, helping the Villagers to promotion to Division One in 1976/77. His biggest haul of tries in a match was three, all his side's tries, in a 13-21 home defeat by Salford on 8 January 1978. Among his contemporaries at Bramley, and a rival for the wing berths, was Peter Goodchild, who he eventually supplanted at Thrum Hall.

As a former gymnast, Keith was exceptionally agile and, like India rubber, he always bounced back. He was a compact 5' 8" and 12st 7lbs, a solid tackler and, in his time at Thrum Hall, possibly the fastest man on the books. He could be very direct and determined and had a nice line in chipping the ball over a defender and regathering – a move which often resulted in tries for himself or his colleagues, or at least caused panic in the opposing defence.

Keith spent six years as Halifax's first-choice left-winger, the first three partnering Dave Cholmondeley. In his 183 games for the

club the only time he played in any other position was at left-centre at Castleford on 19 October 1980. His first full season at Halifax, 1979/80, was most successful. He scored 10 tries in 30 appearances and appeared in his first and only major final, when Halifax lost 6-15 to Leeds at Headingley in the Yorkshire Cup final. Halifax performed brilliantly to reach the semi-finals of the Challenge Cup, losing 7-20 to Hull KR at Leeds with Keith scoring Halifax's only try, going over bravely at the corner in the dying minutes.

Halifax won promotion in 1979/80, and in 1980/81 Keith only missed the final game of the season, which brought to an end a run of sixty-one consecutive appearances. Halifax were unlucky to be relegated but Keith was again in a promotion-winning team in 1981/82. The yo-yo syndrome had hit Halifax, who went down again in 1982/83, when Keith only scored 3 tries, all away from home, in 31 appearances. A third promotion season followed in 1983/84 with Keith having his best return of 17 tries to finish joint leading scorer with right-winger Mick O'Byrne. Playing mostly outside Andy Dickinson, Keith bagged hat-tricks against his former club Bramley at Thrum Hall and at Keighley.

Keith's last season, 1984/85, saw Halifax finally retain their First Division status, as the old order changed from a West Riding-born team to a largely Australian XIII. Most of his final games were played outside Tony Anderson, among them a 17-5 victory at Warrington in the Players Trophy.

# Les White
Second-row forward, 1949-1953

**Previous club:** Wigan

**Halifax debut:** 3 September 1949 v. Liverpool Stanley

**Final Halifax appearance:** 15 August 1953 v. Doncaster

**Appearances:** 120

**Tries:** 30 **Goals:** 0 **Points:** 90

**Transferred to:** Retired

**Honours:** Yorkshire, England, Great Britain

Les White was a second-rower of the highest class, who helped to transform Halifax from also-rans into a trophy-chasing team in a relatively short career at Thrum Hall.

At 5' 11" and 13st 4lbs, Les was not the biggest forward but he had drive, dynamism and that vital ingredient, pure class. He was quick over a distance and had very good acceleration. He was a good handler and an effective leader. He began his career at York and moved to Wigan in 1947 for £1,900, a record for a forward at the time. He had been on tour with the 1946 Indomitables, played in all the tests in Australia and New Zealand and been one of the Lions' major successes. With Wigan he won at Wembley in 1948 and won the Lancashire Cup in 1947, scoring 26 tries in 69 appearances over two seasons.

Les signed for Halifax on 1 September 1949 by which time his value had rocketed to £3,000, the most Halifax had ever paid. He had already played in 6 Tests, 10 internationals and 3 county matches for Yorkshire. Although he was a second-rower, Les played his first four games for Halifax at loose forward. Injury against Hull put Les out after just nine games and he missed the next twenty-one before returning in a 26-8 home defeat of Liverpool Stanley on 11 March 1950, when he scored his first try for the club. Halifax went so well in 1949/50 that they finished fourth in the league, going out in the Championship semi-finals to Wigan after a replay, a personal disappointment to Les, against his former

teammates. Before his injury Les had regained his place in the Yorkshire XIII for both their fixtures.

In 1950/51 Les rattled up 13 tries in 36 games, a post-war best for a forward, while in 1951/52 he was awarded the captaincy. He also won back his England place, scoring a try in England's 35-11 defeat of Wales at St Helens. Les, Stan Kielty and Ken Dean won the County Championship with Yorkshire and played against the Kiwis. Les made a great second-row pairing with Albert Fearnley throughout 1951/52, when he scored 7 tries in 27 appearances.

In 1952/53 Les was in superb form, adding 9 tries to his tally in 39 appearances. On 21 February 1953 he scored a hat-trick in a 32-14 home win over Castleford, the first by a Halifax forward for a decade. Halifax won the Yorkshire League, charged up the league to second and progressed to the Championship final. Les missed the final against St Helens having been injured in a thrilling 18-16 semi-final victory over Bradford Northern at Thrum Hall. Tragically, he only played one more game for Halifax, a knee injury prematurely ending a great career. Halifax received £1,000 insurance money for his loss.

# Colin Whitfield

Full-back, centre, 1986-1990

**Previous club:** Wigan

**Halifax debut:** 22 January 1986 v. Widnes

**Final Halifax appearance:** 8 April 1990 v. Whitehaven

**Appearances:** 128 + 6 subs

**Tries:** 48   **Goals:** 303 + 7 drop goals

**Points:** 805

**Transferred to:** Rochdale Hornets

**Honours:** Lancashire, Great Britain Under-24s, RL Chairman's XIII

Colin Whitfield was probably one of Halifax's most memorable players of the 1980s. Colin was the man who always ran out last, sometimes just making it in time for the kick-off. He was the kicker who often fell over after hitting goals from the touchline. He was the unfortunate victim, probably uniquely, of the insane decision of a referee to sin-bin him at Widnes, when the ball kept maliciously falling over as he tried to place it for a penalty. But he was a good 'un, no question.

Colin was a very quick, elusive and graceful runner – a career record of over a century of tries is ample evidence of that – and an effective tackler and returner of kicks, when he figured at full-back, while he was always liable to do the unexpected. As a goal-kicker, he had a long range. He could be erratic occasionally, missing relatively simple shots and then landing much more difficult goals. It did not seem to unsettle him though, for he booted well over 900 goals in a professional career that spanned the years 1979 to 1993.

He began his career with Salford and moved to Wigan in 1981. At Central Park he was a Lancashire Cup-winner in 1985 and runner-up in 1984, while in 1983 he captained Wigan to a 15-4 victory over Leeds in the Players Trophy final, kicking five goals

(one a drop goal). He also played at Wembley for Wigan in 1984 when they lost to Widnes.

Halifax signed Colin in January 1986 at a club record £25,000, over halfway through the season. He still finished the season as the club's leading scorer with seventy-eight points as Halifax took the Championship. He immediately proved his versatility, playing at centre and wing before taking over from the brilliant Joe Kilroy at full-back.

In 1986/87 Colin broke Tuss Griffiths's club record of 297 points set in 1955/56. His goal at Wigan in a 10-18 Premiership semi-final defeat brought his tally to 298. The previous Saturday he landed three goals in Halifax's 19-18 triumph over St Helens at Wembley. Colin had only failed to score in one of his 40 appearances that season and had been the club's leading try-scorer with 21. At the season's end he spent the summer playing down under with Canterbury-Bankstown.

He was back at Wembley in 1988 but had to settle for a runners-up medal, playing on the left wing against Wigan and kicking two goals. He was once again top points-scorer with 175 in 27 games.

In his last two seasons Colin played most of his rugby at full-back, where he was still a threat. Halifax reached the Yorkshire Cup semi-final in both seasons and in 1990 Colin played his last major final when Halifax again went down to Wigan in the Regal Trophy.

# Jack Wilkinson
Blind-side prop, 1948-1959

**Previous club:** Siddal ARL

**Halifax debut:** 11 October 1948
   *v. Warrington*

**Final Halifax appearance:** 15 April 1959
   *v. Batley*

**Appearances:** 252

**Tries:** 22   **Goals:** 0   **Points:** 66

**Transferred to:** Wakefield Trinity

**Honours:** Rugby League XIII, Yorkshire,
   England, Great Britain

Forwards did not come much harder than Jack Wilkinson – anywhere, anytime! One of the toughest forwards Australia ever produced, hooker Noel Kelly wrote in his autobiography, 'When you start talking "tough" in football, you have to take in the question of balance. The truly tough player is the one who can dish it out, and take it – but still not be deflected from the objective of playing rugby league at the highest level of his ability. And even when you draw those parameters, the field is still a big one – 'Bluey' Wilson, Kevin Ryan, Artie Beetson, Derek Turner, Vince Karalius, Terry Randall, Jack Wilkinson.' Kelly termed that elite group his 'Magnificent Seven'. It is no coincidence that other Australian hardmen of the 1950s and 1960s are on record as having similar views about 'Wilkie'.

No one dropped their guard when Jack was in the opposition. He was relentless, a man determined to master his direct opposite and anyone else who got in the way. Some thought he played the game too vigorously but if he was on your side, there were few complaints. Jack was a six-feet-tall, fifteen-stone hulk of a man, who was a fitness fanatic and had the stamina to match and outlast even the toughest of opponents. He was agile for a big man and he could play good football, despite his reputation. Off the field, he was, like many of the game's bogeymen, extremely affable with an abiding interest in the game and an affection for its traditions and its history.

Jack was arguably the greatest local forward Halifax ever produced. He was born and bred in the town, attended Battinson Road School and played rugby league for Halifax Supporters and Siddal. Halifax signed him aged seventeen in 1948 and he was originally a loose forward. He cost Halifax £300 – £150 down and £150 after six first-team games. He had to wait a couple of years for the latter as he learned his craft in the reserves and did his national service with the RAF Regiment.

By 1952/53 Jack had made the first team as a blind-side prop, although he would occasionally later turn out at second row or loose forward. During that season Halifax finished second in the league and Jack gained his first winners medal, for the Yorkshire League Championship. He also played in his first of many major finals, scoring a try in a 14-24 defeat by St Helens in the Championship final. That Championship-winners medal was the only medal he would fail to obtain, despite playing in five finals (1953, 1954, 1956 with Halifax, 1960 and 1962 with Wakefield).

The 1953/54 season was a magnificent one for Jack. He figured in 43 of Halifax's 48 fixtures, as they topped the table, won the Yorkshire League again and qualified for the Challenge Cup final and the Championship final. After playing in the drawn Wembley final against Warrington, he suffered the disappointment of defeat at Odsal in the replay and at Maine Road. His disappointment was tempered, however, by his first appearance for England against Other Nationalities at Wigan

*Jack Wilkinson goes over the top on a Warrington opponent. Stan Kielty lends a hand to Wilkie.*

on 28 November 1953 and by his selection for the 1954 Australasian tour, when he was almost unbelievably the only Halifax player chosen. On tour Jack made 18 appearances and played in the First Test against Australia and in two against New Zealand. He also made a reputation for himself as one of Britain's most feared forwards in a tour which was marred by controversy. Jack played in the infamous game against New South Wales, which was abandoned because of constant brawling. To be fair to Jack, he played on the wing that afternoon, scoring a try!

In 1954/55 he was in the second row when Hull were beaten 22-14 at Headingley in the Yorkshire Cup final but was in his more usual blind-side prop role the following year when Halifax again beat Hull (7-0) in the final after a replay at Odsal. He had been involved in some of the most hair-raising skirmishes seen on a rugby pitch in the drawn final at Headingley, tales of which are still recounted.

The 1955/56 season also saw him take a third Yorkshire League winners medal and he again appeared in Wembley and Championship finals. The campaign brought him another England cap, an appearance for Britain against France and 3 Tests against New Zealand, in two of which

he scored. He also won the first of his 10 caps for Yorkshire.

Jack's last three seasons at Thrum Hall were less successful, the club only having the 1957/58 Yorkshire League Championship to add to its list of honours. Jack played a couple of games for Rugby League XIIIs against the French and was a tour trialist in 1958. He also shared a successful testimonial with stand-off Ken Dean in his final season, 1958/59, at Halifax. In 1959, even though he was not yet thirty, Halifax decided that his best days were in the past and he was transferred to Wakefield Trinity for £4,500.

History shows that Jack had another five productive years in him. He became a tremendous open-side prop at Belle Vue and played in all Trinity's triumphs of their glory years. He became the first man ever to play in five Wembley finals, gaining winners medals in 1960, 1962 and 1963. He was a Yorkshire Cup winner in 1960 and 1961 and a Yorkshire League winner twice, while he also appeared in unsuccessful Championship finals in 1960 and 1962. Moreover, his international career was resuscitated, as he played in Britain's World Cup-winning team in 1960 and toured again in 1962. His fabulous career ended as captain of Bradford Northern in 1964/65.

# Keith Williams

*Stand-off, winger, 1956-1963*

**Previous club:** Castleford RU

**Halifax debut:** 1 December 1956 v. Blackpool Borough

**Final Halifax appearance:** 26 October 1963 v. Bramley

**Appearances:** 154

**Tries:** 89   **Goals:** 47   **Points:** 361

**Transferred to:** Huddersfield

When Halifax signed Keith Williams for £1,200 from Castleford Rugby Union Club in 1956, it was envisaged that he would eventually take over the stand-off position from Ken Dean, while Bryn Jones would take over the scrum-half spot from Stan Kielty. It did not quite work out like that.

Keith only played 56 of his 154 games for the club at stand-off. Ninety-one were played on the wings, six at centre and one, his last, at full-back. Versatility was one of his main attributes. Keith was not robustly built (5' 8" and about eleven stones) so his game was based on elusiveness, cleverness and speed, all of which he had in abundance. He was a good handler and an effective kicker.

In 1957/58 after only three games at stand-off Keith was drafted in on the right wing, a problem spot following the loss of Arthur Daniels. He was an instant success. In his third game as a winger, on 9 November 1957, he scored eight of Halifax's sixteen tries in a 62-2 home victory over Dewsbury. That performance established a club record that has never been broken. Moreover, no player has scored as many tries in a league fixture since, although Martin Offiah (10), Shaun Edwards (10) and Greg Austin (9) have scored more in knockout competitions.

Later that season he moved over to the left wing, when Johnny Freeman was seriously injured and finished with 40 tries in only 30 games. He created another club record, beaten by only a handful of players anywhere, in scoring tries in eleven consecutive games. That run brought him twenty tries and included three hat-tricks. He collected a Yorkshire League Championship-winners' medal in 1957/58.

In 1958/59 he was again outstanding, scoring 143 points (29 tries, 28 goals) in 38 appearances. Included were six tries against Doncaster in a Yorkshire Cup-tie and four at Dewsbury, while he booted six goals against Hunslet and Huddersfield. He was Halifax's only try-scorer when the Australians won 17-5 at Thrum Hall in 1959.

Keith's scoring rate decreased markedly in the following years, as he played fewer games on the wing. There were no more medals for him, although he did appear on the right wing in Halifax's Challenge Cup semi-final against Wigan in 1961. He also appeared at left-centre in Halifax's dramatic 6-7 home defeat by Hunslet in the Yorkshire Cup semi-final of 1962. His career at Thrum Hall ended in 1963 when he was captain and full-back of the 'A' team, which went on to win the Yorkshire Senior Competition. He scored in all eighteen games he played, none of which were lost, piling up 185 points (85 goals, 5 tries).

Originally a draughtsman, Keith went on to become an Anglican clergyman, serving as rector of Swillington and vicar of Batley.

# David Willicombe
Centre, 1969-1974

**Previous club:** Cardiff IAC RU

**Halifax debut:** 6 September 1969
   *v.* Huddersfield

**Final Halifax appearance:** 6 January 1974
   *v.* Barrow

**Appearances:** 151 + 1 sub

**Tries:** 54  **Goals:** 26  **Points:** 214

**Transferred to:** Wigan

**Honours:** Other Nationalities (county),
   Wales, Great Britain

Cardiff-born David Willicombe joined Halifax aged eighteen in 1969 and quickly became a fine centre. He had been signed from the Cardiff International Athletic Club (the famous Kyaks) which produced Johnny Freeman and Billy Boston. His fee was £1,500, which Halifax would more than recoup.

Ideally built for the centre, at six feet and 13st 7lbs, Willicombe had bags of pace, a disconcerting swerve and the ability to power through gaps. He was capable of running in long-distance tries but could also send his winger away once he had punctured defences. In less than five years at Thrum Hall David exhibited genuine class and was a worthy successor to such centres as Tommy Lynch, John Burnett and Geoff Palmer.

In his first two seasons he generally played at left-centre alongside his compatriot David Jones, although he did occasionally figure on the wing and once at stand-off. So rapid was his progress that within five months of his debut, he had played for Wales in a 15-11 victory over France at Perpignan. His second season, 1970/71, saw him bag 15 tries in 32 matches, while the following season he played a massive 44 games, which included starring roles in Halifax's drive to the John Player Trophy final victory over Wakefield Trinity. David was a try-scorer in the final but had already scored crucial tries in the 5-3 victory over York in the second round and in the 36-13 third-round triumph over Barrow.

In 1972/73 David claimed sixteen tries and also filled in as a competent goal-kicker, landing twenty-three, including five-goal hauls at home and away against Hunslet. The following season revealed him at his best, despite the fact that Halifax were playing in the Second Division. Great Britain selected him for his Test debut on 20 January 1974, when he was a try-scorer in a 24-5 win over France at Grenoble. His winger, Keith Fielding, grabbed a hat-trick. By that time, however, David was on Halifax's transfer list and soon signed for Wigan. The fee was a huge £9,000. A few weeks after his transfer, David was selected for the 1974 Lions tour, playing in Britain's 20-0 Third Test victory over New Zealand.

David Willicombe's representative career brought him 3 Test caps and 13 Welsh caps, including the 1975 Wales World Championship tour. He would have won more caps but for a succession of broken arms in his time with Wigan. Those injuries forced his retirement at the age of twenty-nine in 1980. He played 119 games for Wigan, amassing 120 points (36 tries, 6 goals) but had only runners-up medals from the Lancashire Cup finals of 1977 and 1980 to show for six years at Central Park.

While a Halifax player David worked as a maintenance electrician at United Biscuits at Ovenden but later became a publican.

# Scott Wilson
Winger, centre, 1982-1989

**Previous club:** Brighouse Rangers ARL

**Halifax debut:** 22 August 1982 v. Leeds

**Final Halifax appearance:** 16 April 1989
   v. St Helens

**Appearances:** 91 + 10 subs

**Tries:** 18   **Goals:** 0   **Points:** 72

**Transferred to:** Retired

Scott Wilson was one of the newcomers brought to Halifax by coach Ken Roberts at the start of the 1982/83 season. A nineteen-year-old from Brighouse, Scott spent most of that season playing for the reserves, scoring 6 tries in 23 games, split between stand-off and centre. He made his first-team debut at left-centre to Keith Waites in the opening game, a 10-39 thrashing by Leeds at Headingley. His next game in the firsts was the last game of the season, an even more disastrous defeat – 2-47 to Castleford at Thrum Hall.

Scott appeared to be doomed to reserve-team football. The 1983/84 season brought him just 2 first-team appearances as a substitute and none at all in 1984/85. Then in 1985/86 he suddenly snared a first-team place, when he was called into the side to play right-winger in a Yorkshire Cup-tie against Castleford. Thirty-two consecutive games followed, initially as a winger but then at left-centre, first to Brian Juliff and latterly to Wilf George. Scott scored five tries in that period, his two match-winning efforts against Hull at Thrum Hall being the most memorable.

Scott was typical of the unfashionable Halifax team which took the Championship in 1985/86. He was not star material. At 5' 10" and twelve stones, he was not a big man, nor was he particularly fast or elusive. He was, however, enthusiastic, reliable, good in defence and quick to cover for other players' mistakes. Crucially, he made very few mistakes himself. At the close of the 1985/86 campaign Scott was moved to left wing, after Wilf George suffered a broken jaw, and played in all the Premiership rounds including the final against Warrington at Elland Road.

The 1986/87 season was even more memorable. Scott was in the side which beat Castleford 9-8 in the Charity Shield in Douglas and scored 8 tries in 34 appearances. Most of his games were played as right-winger after he displaced Eddie Riddlesden at the end of October. He figured in that position against the Australians and was there throughout Halifax's run to Wembley, scoring a try in 'Fax's magnificent 35-7 third round victory over Hull KR. Few 'Fax fans who saw the final against St Helens will forget the sight of a heavily bloodied Scott Wilson parading round the pitch with the Challenge Cup.

Season 1987/88 brought Scott another appearance in the Charity Shield and a couple of outings at stand-off but only ten appearances overall. His last campaign, 1988/89, yielded 20 appearances, including two in the second-row at Leeds on Boxing Day and at home to Castleford. On 23 October 1988 he was a try-scorer from the left wing, when Halifax beat France 24-18 on a unique short tour by the Chanticleers. His last game was a remarkable 40-8 victory over St Helens at Thrum Hall.

# Alan Wood

Utility forward, 1972-1980

**Previous club:** Dewsbury Celtic ARL

**Halifax debut:** 24 October 1972 v. Wigan
BBC2 Floodlit Trophy

**Final Halifax appearance:** 28 September
1980 v. Widnes

**Appearances:** 95 + 20 subs

**Tries:** 5   **Goals:** 0   **Points:** 15

**Transferred to:** Keighley (1), Huddersfield (2)

For sheer endeavour and hard work it would be hard to find a better forward than Alan Wood. A supremely fit player, Woody always gave every game everything he had. He had two spells at Thrum Hall, where he forged a reputation as a ferocious, hard-tackling dynamo, who could play anywhere in the pack. In his first period with the club he tended to be used in the second row, while in his later days blind-side prop was his most likely position.

Alan was signed from Dewsbury Celtic for £250 as a hooker or second-rower. His first-team debut, at Wigan, however, saw him enter the fray as a half-time substitute for loose forward John Martin. After making several appearances as a substitute he got his first start at hooker on 30 December 1972 in a 12-17 home defeat by Leeds, when he was propped by Terry Fogerty and Terry Dewhirst, in a stormy encounter which saw Bruce Burton's jaw broken.

Alan made 25 appearances in the promotion season of 1973/74 but the following season 'Fax were relegated and entered a steep decline. Alan made only 16 appearances in his last two seasons but finally got his name among the try-scorers in a 20-10

home defeat of Hull on 24 August 1975. In January 1976 he was exchanged for Keighley prop Laurie Hinchliffe, having last played in a 12-14 home defeat by Bramley on 30 November 1975. Shortly after joining Keighley he was in the side which won 13-9 at Halifax in the first round of the Challenge Cup and figured in their Challenge Cup semi-final against St Helens at Fartown, when Saints scraped home 5-4.

While with Keighley Alan played as an amateur for Dewsbury Celtic, enjoying a fine season in 1977/78, when he was Man of the Match in Celtic's 13-7 BARLA Yorkshire Cup final victory over NDLB (Hull) at Batley. A few months later on the same ground he was in the Celtic team which lost 5-15 to Wigan in the first round of the Challenge Cup, being sent off in the last minute.

The Mount Pleasant ground was also the scene of his reappearance in Halifax's colours on 20 August 1978, when Halifax knocked Batley out in the first round of the Yorkshire Cup 24-8. Maurice Bamford had brought him back to Thrum Hall as Halifax strove to recover former glories. Alan had had a reputation in his earlier days for his fieriness and Halifax fans were a bit dubious about his return. They need not have worried – the fire remained but his discipline was exemplary and it is worth recording that Alan was never sent off in his entire career with Halifax, either in the firsts or 'A' team. He was a magnificent performer in the team which won promotion, reached the Yorkshire Cup final and the Cup semi-final in 1979/80.